133.1 Anderson, Jean
AND
    The haunting of
       America

DATE			
1-18-79	5-10-83		
1-25-79	10-19-83		
3-8-79	1-24-04		
3-15-79	11-2-84		
4-19-79	4-16-84		
5-3-79	10-12-87		
11-6-79	8-10-04		
2-5-80			
4-15-80			
4/30/80			
4-27-80			
1-6-82			

The Haunting of America

JEAN ANDERSON

The Haunting
of America

Ghost Stories from Our Past

Illustrated by Eric von Schmidt

HOUGHTON MIFFLIN COMPANY BOSTON

Grateful acknowledgment is made to the editors of
Today's Girl for permission to reprint "The Silver Doe,"
which appeared in the October 1971 issue.

The author also wishes to thank the following publishers for permission to reprint the quotations listed below:

Harcourt Brace Jovanovich, Inc., for the excerpts on pages 44–45 from *Myths After Lincoln* by Lloyd Lewis, Copyright 1929.

Evans Publishing Company, for the quotations on pages 43–44, and page 45 from *Abraham Lincoln Returns* by Harriett M. Shelton, © 1957.

The Macmillan Publishing Company, Inc., for the selection on page 48 from the poem "Abraham Lincoln Walks at Midnight," *The Collected Poems of Vachel Lindsay*, by Vachel Lindsay, Copyright 1914 by Macmillan Publishing Company, Inc., copyright renewed 1942 by Elizabeth C. Lindsay.

From PROMINENT AMERICAN GHOSTS by Susy Smith, Copyright © 1967 by Susy Smith. With permission of Thomas Y. Crowell Company, Inc.

Mrs. Chester W. Jeffries, for the passages on pages 51–53, and the Orrery Manuscript Harvard College Library, for the passage on page 54 from *Another Secret Diary of William Byrd of Westover for the Years 1739–1741, Part II*, edited by Maude H. Woodfin, decoded by Marion Tinling, Dietz Press, Inc., Richmond, Virginia, copyright 1942.

In Acknowledgment

I should like to thank, in particular, the following persons who gave generously of their time and provided valuable assistance and information used in the preparation of this book: Elizabeth W. Bagby, Charles City, Virginia; John W. Cornelison, Research Historian, Wyoming State Archives and Historical Department; Joe Faith, Director of Information, State of Missouri, Division of Commerce and Industrial Development; Bruce Crane Fisher, Westover, Charles City, Virginia; Jean Todd Freeman, English Department, University of Southern Mississippi, Hattiesburg; Donald R. Mathewson, Public Information Officer, former State of Delaware; Marjie Mugno, *Texas Highways;* Russell W. Peterson, Governor of Delaware; Alton H. Slagle, New York *Daily News;* Marian B. Smith, Cloquet, Minnesota; E. Berkeley Tompkins, Director, Division of Historical and Cultural Affairs, State of Delaware; Conrad F. Weitzel, Reference Librarian, The Ohio Historical Society; Martha E. Wright, Reference Librarian, Indiana State Library; and a special thanks to Pamela V. Kobbé for helping research, type and proofread.

For Linda and Donald and Kim

Contents

Contents

Preface

$\mathcal{M}$*ention* "ghosts" or "spirits" or "tricks of the supernatural" and a castle springs to mind — a Macbethian castle, of course, brooding in the Scottish Highlands. Or an Irish abbey where the Angelus peals mysteriously under the hand of an invisible bell ringer. Or a fog-shrouded English great house set upon a land's end promontory high above the sea.

But America, too, has its ghosts. Not just the everyday run of poltergeists, rappings and materializations (although there are dozens of these). But stellar ghosts as well. Spirits of departed presidents, for example. Or apparitions encountered by living presidents. Ghosts of celebrated houses. Ghosts connected with historic events. Ghosts that characterize in some way the life and times of a particular region. Ghosts that have become a part of American legend.

Not every state can claim a ghost. The Plains and Rocky Mountain states are singularly lacking. ("Must be the clear air out here," quipped one state historian in reply to a query about ghosts. "Seems to be bad for ec-

In Memory of
Deacon Daniel
Davis who died
June 2[?] th[?]

[...] Memory [...]
M[?]s T[...]
wife [...]
[...] 1761 [...]
Year of her age
Buried in Killingly
M[?] Hezekiah Davis
died [...] of Chester
Oct[?] [...] 1776 in [...]

toplasm".) But if these areas run short on psychic phenomena, the East and South more than compensate. These two regions are America's most heavily haunted (perhaps because of their Anglo-Saxon heritage). The task here is not in finding a ghost, but in deciding *which* ghost makes the best story.

Not every ghostly appearance, obviously, *is* a story. Indeed, some of the more interesting possibilities proved to be nothing more than unrelated, fleeting incidents. Of "iffy" happenings based upon hearsay. Moreover, some of the ghosts were (you'll excuse it) "deadly" dull. Henry David Thoreau's mother, for example, who bustled about the Louisa May Alcott house in Concord, Massachusetts (the house originally belonged to the Thoreaus), dusting furniture, putting out hearth fires, because the Alcotts themselves were too absorbed with their papers to take care of the house. A busy ghost, but a boring one, too.

In Alexandria, Virginia, the children of Robert E. Lee are said to romp in an upstairs room of the house Lee owned as a young man. Farther south, the raven-haired spirit of Theodosia Burr drifts over the dunes of Hatteras Island where the beautiful young Miss Burr was shipwrecked. The ghost of her father, Aaron Burr, has been reported skulking about New York's Greenwich Village. Shadowing Alexander Hamilton's ghost? (It, too, has been seen in the Village). People living along New York's Bowery say they sometimes hear the clip-clop of old "Peg-Leg" Peter Stuyvesant and those up the Hudson River near West Point swear that whenever the night turns dark and stormy "Mad Anthony"

Wayne is sure to go galloping. Fascinating reports, all. But too fragmentary to hang stories on.

The purpose of this book is to single out some two dozen of the more interesting *full-fledged* American ghost stories, particularly those involving the apparitions of famous Americans, the ghosts that haunt landmark houses, and the legendary (or maybe-not-so-legendary) spirits that emerged during — and are representative of — America's infancy, adolescence and adulthood.

No attempt whatever has been made to "chase" or communicate with ghosts, to establish contact "with the other side." Nor has there been any effort to verify or explain any ghostly phenomena. The intent, simply, is to set down some of the stories that have been told time and again around hearths and campfires at night, that have spellbound each new generation of Americans.

Some of the stories have become classics — Ocean-Born Mary and the Bell Witch of Tennessee, to name two. But the majority, equally amusing or compelling, are known locally only: the eerie giant Jack-O-Lantern of Devil's Promenade in southwestern Missouri, for example, that rollicks down the highway at dusk . . . the Gray Man of Pawleys Island, South Carolina, seen before every major hurricane . . . and in Hawaii that other messenger of doom, Madame Pele, who appears before each volcanic eruption to warn those who have been kind to her.

The ghostly personalities profiled here are as varied as the eras and areas they haunt. Some are rambunctious poltergeists hurling eggs, dishes, knives and furniture. Some are benign spirits who come to sit or chat.

Others are vengeful, returning to right a wrong, and still others are mournful reincarnated animals, howling or stalking through the night.

Some of the ghosts date back to America's earliest beginnings — to Sir Walter Raleigh's "Lost Colony." Others are thoroughly twentieth century. Together they span America's growing-up years. They span, too, America's length and breadth, and in so doing, emerge as a sort of unofficial guide to "Ghostly Americana."

JEAN ANDERSON

New York, New York

The Haunting of America

The Golden Girl
of Appledore Island

It was a sky-blue morning, one of those eerily calm days that too seldom visit the ragged Isles of Shoals ten miles at sea off the coast of New Hampshire.

The young newspaperman, vacationing on the island of Appledore, had risen early and hiked to a long, low-lying point to catch the sunrise. Sea, land and sky seemed in motionless repose. The ocean, which in wintry rage had driven ships against the rocks of Appledore, splintering them into kindling, showed not the merest ripple. No cloud sailed the sky. No breeze fingered the rockweed. No green crabs danced in tidal pools. No gulls wheeled overhead.

It was as though time — life — were frozen. Suspended in a nether land.

Suddenly, with no warning at all, she stood beside him — so close he could have reached out and taken her arm. She seemed oblivious of his presence and stood entranced, staring seaward. She was young, twenty perhaps, startlingly beautiful, with a cascade

of golden hair that touched her waist. Her dress was filmy, white, as though woven of cobwebs. She had slipped up so silently, materialized, almost, out of the dawn. Probably the wife of a young fisherman, the reporter decided. Or perhaps a fiancée.

"Do you see him?" he asked the girl, scanning the horizon for the silhouette of a fishing smack.

She spun round. He had never seen eyes so blue or so sad. "He will come again," she murmured, then disappeared behind a boulder as noiselessly as she had come, her feet seeming to float above the ground.

A chill seized the reporter; for an instant he shuddered. Had he seen the girl? She seemed so unreal. So vaporous. Still, she had spoken. He was certain of that.

As a newspaperman working on one of the nearby mainland villages, he had heard of odd happenings on the Isles of Shoals. The islands were rife with legend, indeed had the very look of legend, as if some prehistoric giant, in a surge of temper, had scooped up a handful of rocky New England coast and hurled it into the sea. Even the names of the seven islands had a storybook quality — Appledore, Cedar, Duck and Smuttynose, which belonged to the State of Maine; Londoner's, Star and White, which were a part of New Hampshire.

Dozens of lives had been lost in these islands down the years: fishermen caught in a sudden storm (the islands' name comes not from their rocky shoals, although these most certainly exist, but from the "shoals" or schools of fish that swim there); cargo ships blown from the sealanes into island shallows; pirate ships, slipping too close to shore.

Spirits of the dead walked these islands.

And what of the girl? Could one so lovely be a ghost? She had appeared out of thin air. And dissolved into it, easily as a morning mist. The ground she had walked seemed untouched, the shells there were uncrushed.

A melancholy settled over the newspaperman. The "golden girl" drifted in and out of his dreams, dominated his thoughts by day, lured him again and again to the point. He returned there each morning at dawn. And the lady came on the silent breath of early morning, garbed as before in white, her hair shimmering in the sun. Each appearance was the same. She arrived suddenly, silently to stare at the horizon. Then she would turn, fix soulful eyes upon him and whisper,

"He *will* come again."

Her words were always the same and the reporter was uncertain now that she actually spoke. He heard them, to be sure, but in his ear or in his mind's eye?

Obsessed now by her visits, the reporter began inquiring about the girl. None of the islanders knew her or knew anyone who knew her. Then, in a remote part of the island, he met an old fisherman who not only knew of the "golden lady" but had actually seen her a time or two on the point at dawn.

"Comes only at dawn of a clear day," he said. "Comes only to that point."

She wasn't an islander but the lady love of one of Blackbeard's captains. She had been put ashore on the point to guard a treasure he had buried there. The captain had promised to return — for the girl and for the treasure.

But he never did. He was killed at sea.

Blackbeard! The reporter gasped. That ferocious pirate had plundered the Atlantic seaboard from the West Indies to Canada, terrorizing virtually everyone who lived within the sound of the surf and leaving, in the wake of cruelty, scores of legends of buried treasure.

So here was another treasure. With a "golden ghost" to guard it. The girl was indeed a ghost, for this was the year 1826. Blackbeard, the reporter knew, had been captured and beheaded some hundred years earlier just off North Carolina's Outer Banks.

And what of the "golden girl" today, almost a hundred and fifty years after the young reporter's brush with the nether world? Does she stand yet on the low point of Appledore Island, guarding the gold buried there two and a half centuries ago?

Some islanders say so. That if the morning is

calm, the sea glassy and the sun golden, she will appear fleetingly. They say, too, that she will continue to appear until her lover returns.

Who is to know? One day, maybe, he *will* return.

Ocean-Born Mary

In 1720, after a long, wallowing voyage from Londonderry, Ireland, a shipload of immigrants neared the Massachusetts shore. The Irishmen, together with their families, were bound for Londonderry, New Hampshire, where they intended to settle and build new lives. Theirs had not been a particularly hazardous voyage as voyages in the age of sail often were. Still, they had endured weeks of heavy seas, crowded foul-smelling quarters and spartan rations.

With the sea now calm and America almost within sight, spirits lifted and snatches of ballads were hummed and whistled above and below decks. The immigrants were relieved that their crossing was very nearly over; they were eager to be ashore and to begin afresh in a new land. That very day a baby girl had been born aboard ship, a bonny colleen with enormous blue-green eyes and a full head of red hair. She was the daughter of the ship's captain and his bride, a good omen surely that things would go well.

Suddenly there appeared on the horizon the shad-

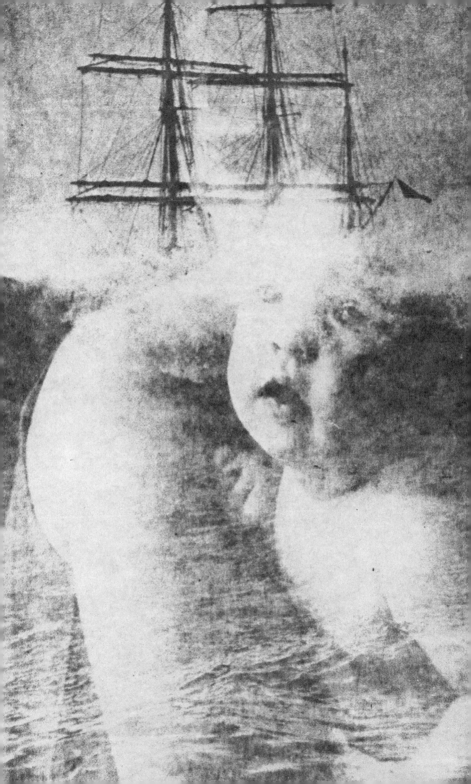

owy outline of a ship. A square-rigger she was, in full sail, and she sliced through the sea with sword-stroke speed. She flew no colors, failed to answer the immigrant ship's signal, but bore down, then fired a gun straight across the ship's bow. The Irishmen fell to their knees in terror and prayer.

Their luck had run out. Swaggering across the bridge of the frigate was a mustachioed pirate, his skin burned cinnamon by the sun. He ordered a dinghy put out, then easily, catlike, slipped down the rope into the bobbing boat. A small party joined him and together they crossed over to the Irish ship and swung aboard.

"I am Captain Pedro," he announced. Though swarthy and dark, the pirate spoke impeccable English. He ordered the immigrants to line up and be shot. He was commandeering the ship and whatever cargo she held. Then, just as his men, with pistols raised, were ready to fire, the newborn baby let out a piercing wail. Captain Pedro jerked around, signaled his men to hold their fire, and dashed below decks. In the captain's quarters he found the red-headed infant suckling her mother. Something within him softened.

"What is her name?" he asked.

"None as yet," the mother replied.

"Then, Madame, if you will grant me the favor of naming this baby girl after my own mother, I will

harm neither this ship nor her passengers." The
mother consented only too happily.

"Her name shall be Mary," Captain Pedro replied
gently.

With that he was gone, as abruptly as he had
come. He swung into the dinghy, crossed to his own
ship, vanished below decks, then bounded topside
again. The Irishmen gasped as they watched him
slither into the dinghy and make once more for their
ship. Brushing past the kneeling immigrants, Captain
Pedro hurried below decks and burst into the captain's cabin.

"Here, Madame," he said, laying a bolt of embroidered green silk on the bed. "For little Mary's wed-
ding gown."

With that he was gone — from the captain's cabin,
from the Irish ship, and finally from view. The
Irishmen were incredulous. The baby Mary, ocean-
born, was indeed a good omen.

Next day the ship docked safely in Boston Harbor
and the immigrants set out on the overland journey
to Londonderry in the hills of New Hampshire. All,
that is, except the captain, his wife and baby. They
remained in Boston. They had barely settled when
the captain fell ill and died, leaving his young widow
and baby daughter alone in a strange land.

The young widow decided to follow her ship-
mates to New Hampshire. She found them easily,
settled into the community and set about rearing

"Ocean-Born Mary," as the immigrants had nick-named the child. The whole town watched with pride as Mary grew first into a little girl with rollick-ing red curls and green, laughing eyes, then into a young woman of awesome beauty. Mary was unusu-ally tall, very nearly six feet, and her presence was that of a goddess. Wherever she went, she turned heads, and beaus for miles around vied for her hand.

Mary married early, wearing a gown made of the green embroidered silk Captain Pedro had given her mother. Within less than ten years she had borne four red-headed sons and, like her mother before her, been widowed at a very young age.

Unbeknownst to her at the time, Captain Pedro, now an aging man, had retired from his life of bucca-neering and was building at nearby Henniker, New Hampshire, a stately home high on a hill at the end of an allée, beyond the sound of the sea, beyond the sight of any other house. Solitude is what Captain Pedro now sought. And companionship.

He had inquired as to the whereabouts of young Mary and he intended now to contact her. Mary knew, of course, the story of Captain Pedro. She had heard it many times from her mother. But to her it was little more than a fairytale.

So when Captain Pedro arrived one day at her door, introduced himself and shook hands, she all but swooned. He seemed, however, a kindly man, fa-therly almost (certainly a pirate who would forfeit a

sturdy ship simply for the honor of naming a newborn girl wasn't altogether heartless). In the days
that followed, Captain Pedro came often to call. He
toured Mary and her four sons about the countryside, then drove them up to Henniker to see the magnificent Colonial home his ship's carpenters were
building. Mary was impressed.

"Come and live with me and bring the boys," he
begged Mary. "I am old now. I have not much
longer to live. I need someone to look after me. By
the same token, you and your sons need caring for. I
will see that you lack nothing."

Mary accepted and moved to Henniker. She
served Captain Pedro well and he, in turn, lavished
gifts upon her and her sons. One day he presented
Mary a handsome coach-and-four that delighted her
so she was seen daily, almost, driving with her sons
into the rumpled hills above Henniker.

Captain Pedro spent most of his time in the big
Colonial house or in the rear garden. He occasionally made trips down to Boston or to Portsmouth or,
as he said, "down to see the sea."

Mary never questioned him about these jaunts.
Nor did she question him ever about the midnight
he stole home in the company of a rough-voiced
man. They seemed to be carrying something heavy
— a chest, perhaps — and they made their way un-
steadily into the rear garden. Presently Mary heard
the sound of digging — shovels striking packed

earth, glancing off stones, scraping, squeaking. There followed a heavy thud, as though something weighty had been lowered into a deep hole, then a low agonizing howl of pain, then more shoveling. It was daybreak before the captain came to bed. He made no mention the next day of the midnight digging, or of the gravel-voiced confrere.

About a year after the garden incident, Mary came home from a drive to find the house deserted. She called to the captain and, hearing no answer, raced into the garden. There she found him lying in a puddle of blood. His throat had been slit by a cutlass.

Mary remained calm. She knew what to do because the captain had instructed her. She was to bury him underneath the hearthstone in the kitchen — it measured eight feet long, three feet wide, and the space underneath was just big enough for a man's body. With the help of her sons, Mary laid Captain Pedro to rest as he had wished, then rolled the heavy stone back in place and sealed the cracks.

After the captain's murder, Mary lived on at the house on the hill. One by one her sons, now quite grown up, left to fight the Revolution. No one about the town of Henniker appeared to miss Captain Pedro. Or to inquire as to his whereabouts. Mary, of course, volunteered no information. Standing as it did, aloof from its neighbors, the captain's house beckoned few visitors. Mary loved the house he had built, the way its stair resembled that of a ship, the way its floors cambered like decks. She never felt alone there.

As the years passed, Mary became more and more of a hermit. And a legend around town. People began to talk about strange doings at the house on the hill, about the crazy old woman who lived there. These gossips had never known Mary. They were the grandsons and granddaughters, great-grandsons and great-granddaughters, great-great-grandsons and great-great-granddaughters of her contemporaries. Mary had outlived them every one.

She was so old now the town of Henniker began to think her immortal. But in the end, she too died. It was the year 1814 and Mary was ninety-four years old. All four of her sons had predeceased her.

With no inheritors, the house on the hill fell derelict. First the curious came to have a look at the house a pirate captain had built, the treasure hunters followed, reasoning that a pirate would surely have buried gold there; then, inevitably, the vandals. They stoned the windows and jimmied the doors. Then, as abruptly as they had descended upon the old house, the vandals vanished. The house stood idle, a gothic pile, brooding, forbidding, the very picture of a haunted house. Weeds ran amok in the garden, brambles claimed the hill and closed the drive. Even the sheltering trees seemed twisted and spectral, charred skeletons dancing in the wind.

Stories began to circulate on the streets of Henniker . . . of lights appearing in the windows at night . . . of the shadow of a tall, haggard woman moving through the rooms at dusk . . . of a flaming-haired beauty descending the central stair . . . of a coach-and-four galloping silently up the drive . . . of agonizing groans in the garden.

Eventually the house was sold. Several times, in fact, the last sale being transacted fairly recently. The present owners seem happy in the old house on the hill, but they do admit to "strange noises." Weary footsteps pacing one of the bedrooms . . . knocks at doors . . . doorknobs squeakily turning. They admit, too, that their dog, an unusually amenable animal, senses something sinister about the cellar. He refuses to go there, backs off from the cellar door, snarling, with his hair standing on end.

Only a few years ago a state trooper patrolling a highway below the house saw a tall, red-haired woman walking toward him down the road. Nothing odd in that — *except* that she was wearing Colonial dress.

And at about that same time, a medium, strangely attracted to the house, went there to see if she could establish contact with the Beyond. Her knock at the door was answered by a tall, red-haired woman in Colonial costume. The medium's sixth sense warned her not to enter. She didn't that day. But the next day she returned, and this time her knock was answered by an altogether different person, the mistress of the house. When told about the red-headed woman, she replied,

"But that is impossible. There was no one here yesterday."

Who, then, was the red-haired woman?

Ocean-Born Mary?

The Lady in Black of Boston Harbor

She walks yet in Boston Harbor, the gallant Lady in Black. No one can predict when she will appear. Or why. Or what her mood will be. She is sometimes sprightly, sometimes dolorous, sometimes haughty, sometimes humble.

Who is she? How did she come to haunt Fort Warren, a somber military garrison on the rocky outcropping of George's Island seven miles at sea in Boston Harbor?

It all began a little over a hundred years ago at the outset of the Civil War, not in Boston but in the little town of Crawfordville in the red, mud-baked hills of northeast Georgia. A young lieutenant there, Andrew Lanier, had been called up. Nothing very unusual in that. Thousands of southern youths were being conscripted. Lieutenant Lanier, however, was to have married his childhood sweetheart within the month. Rather than wait until his first leave, or until the end of the war, he begged his intended to marry him at once.

She agreed and the two were married in a simple ceremony. They spent forty-eight hours together, then Lieutenant Lanier joined his division and rode off to fight "The War for Southern Independence," as Southerners preferred to call the Civil War.

In less than a month, he was captured and taken as prisoner of war to the Corridor of Dungeons at Fort Warren in Boston Harbor along with some six hundred other Confederates. He wrote his wife a long letter explaining what had happened although he never expected the letter to reach her.

It did reach her and her reaction, on reading the news, startled both her family and friends. They gathered around, overflowing with sympathy. But sympathy was not what she sought. It was support for a bold and reckless plan, a scheme so daring few men would have undertaken it.

Young Mrs. Lanier was a lady far ahead of her time, decidedly not a frail southern gentlewoman fluttering a fan or sniffing smelling salts at the onset of each sinking spell. Nor was she one to languish about the house, bemoaning her fate.

Her decision was immediate. She would go to Boston, visit her husband, try everything within her power to secure his release. Her family and friends were aghast. Vainly they tried to reason with her. Did she not realize how perilous such a journey would be? And how futile any attempts to see her husband?

No amount of reasoning or arguing or cajoling could dissuade her. She *would* go, she vowed. She arranged for passage aboard a blockade runner that would put her ashore near the elbow of Cape Cod. She had friends there, Southern sympathizers, who would help her travel north to Boston and carry out her plan.

Two and a half months later she was at Hull within full view of Fort Warren. Eager as she was to be reunited with her husband, she made her plans slowly and carefully. With a telescope she studied Fort Warren in detail, noting the position of its Corridor of Dungeons where her husband was incarcerated. She noted, too, the sentry posts, the paths the guards patrolled, the height of the prison walls and their distance from the shore.

Finally, on a blustery January night, she was ready to set out. Friends rowed her across Hingham Bay into Boston Harbor, and then through black, roller-coastering swells to George's Island. She had shorn her hair and donned a dark man's suit, the easier to scale the prison walls and slip undetected through the night.

Once ashore, she crouched in the surf, waiting for the sentries to pass out of sight. She clocked their patrol once again to make sure she had not miscalculated. From the time the two men met, passed one another, disappeared, then turned and reappeared, she had exactly a minute and a half. In those ninety seconds she must slip from the shore to the bushes massed around the base of the fort, a distance of two, perhaps three hundred feet. Once there, she would wait for the sentries to pass again, then in that minute and a half, scramble over the walls into the courtyard by the Corridor of Dungeons.

Stinging-cold pebbles of sleet rattled down. But she welcomed the sleet because its sounds would muffle her own and its slanting, silvery fall would provide a curtain of camouflage. Moreover, the guards were not apt to tarry on a night so raw. Nor were they likely to expect an intruder.

All went well. She stole during the first minute and a half across the grounds to the shelter of the shrubbery, then in the second minute and a half clambered up the rough stone walls and dropped with a plop no louder than that of an apple falling from a tree into the courtyard by the Corridor of Dungeons. There were no sentries in sight.

She stood now, after so many months, within a few feet of her husband. Only the prison wall separated them. She examined it and saw that not ten feet above, there was a long narrow slit. With luck, the signal she had planned would be heard.

There was a folk tune the two of them had sung since childhood. She would whistle a few bars. Her husband, she knew, would recognize it and whistle a reply.

But no answering whistle came. She heard only

the rustle of sleet. Suddenly, for the first time during the entire hazardous scheme, terror clutched at her heart. What if her husband had died? Or been transferred to another prison? There was no way the news could have reached her.

She whistled again, more shrilly this time, but heard only the frantic beatings of her heart. Then it came, muffled, as if from the depths of a well, the next few bars of the song.

Her husband had heard. He was safe. Again he whistled the snatch of tune, and when she looked up toward the opening in the wall she saw snaking down from it a twist of bedding. She grabbed hold, was pulled up to the slit, then shimmied through. The next instant she was in her husband's arms, trembling and tearful.

He was incredulous. How had she slipped through enemy lines and reached Boston? How had she crossed Boston Harbor to Fort Warren? How had she evaded the guards and stolen *inside* Fort Warren?

She told her story, not only to her husband, but to as many of his confederates as could crowd around. Then she produced the bundle that she had carried so protectively all the way from Crawfordville, Georgia. In it lay a pick, a shovel, a pistol and a box of bullets.

Her plan had been to help her husband escape. But the prisoners now hit upon a far more dazzling scheme. They would tunnel not out of the prison but into the parade ground near the keep. There they would emerge, catch the guard off duty, seize the armory and then the fort itself. Once Fort Warren had been taken, they would train its guns on Boston, and very possibly change the entire course of the war.

Week by week, inch by inch, the prisoners dug their tunnel, scattering bits of dirt onto the ground outside the fortress walls, but hiding more of it in their blankets and rolled-up shirts. At last they reached their mark, the center of the parade ground from which they would stage their attack on the armory. But as the pick swung up, it struck not earth, then air, but the wall of the keep. At the crunch of metal on stone, the guard spun around. He knew instantly what had happened. Troops were summoned and sent, on the double, to the Corridor of Dungeons.

Just minutes from victory, the Confederates were doomed. One by one they were led onto the parade ground and counted. Eleven prisoners were missing, including Lieutenant Lanier.

The eleven were quickly found, however, once the tunnel entrance was located, and ordered to show themselves. "You might as well come out and surrender," the garrison's colonel commanded. "You have failed."

The eleven holdouts crawled from the tunnel, but

not before a final desperate plan had been agreed upon. The Union soldiers knew nothing of Mrs. Lanier. And therein lay their hope.

When all of the prisoners had been led to the parade ground and accounted for, she would slip up behind the colonel, pistol cocked, and demand that he surrender the fort. The Confederates knew that he would do no such thing but, they reasoned, in the instant that he was caught off guard, they could turn upon their captors, disarm them and take the fort.

But it did not work out that way. The colonel, instead of being rattled by the surprise attack, coolly motioned his troops to circle around the "mystery man in black." Shivering, less for fear of her own life than for fear that this plan, too, would fail, Mrs. Lanier stood valiantly, watching the ring of blue tighten about her. Then more quickly, it seemed, than a copperhead could strike, the colonel snatched her pistol. It misfired, spattering shrapnel everywhere. One jagged piece caught Lieutenant Lanier in the temple and he fell, mortally wounded.

Mrs. Lanier crumpled to the ground beside her husband, sobbing hysterically. Only then did the Union troops discover the identity of the "mystery man in black" and hear her incredible, courageous love story. Few among them were untouched by the young bride's story. And yet she was a spy and, as such, must be hanged.

"One last request," she begged of the colonel. "I

am weary of the men's clothes I wear. Let me go to my hanging dressed as a lady."

The colonel granted the request. He had the fort searched for fabric, then presented the young bride with a black robe that had been used in amateur theatricals. From it Mrs. Lanier fashioned a makeshift gown.

On the morning of February 2, 1862, she walked to the gallows, wearing the black gown she had made and a faint, fleeting smile. That afternoon, the troops cut her body down and laid it to rest in a grave beside that of her husband.

Her spirit, however, did not rest. Seven weeks after the hanging, in the deep of night, a sentry felt two hands around his throat . . . tightening . . . tightening . . . tightening . . . he wheeled about and, to his horror, saw standing there a lady in black bathed in miasmic light, her smile seeming to drift upon the air. It was Mrs. Andrew Lanier.

In the beginning, the soldiers scoffed at the story. But then, one by one, others of them were visited by the Lady in Black as they stood guard duty. Her appearances were no longer taken lightly. Nor have they been in ensuing years. (During World War II she so startled a young sentry that he remains to this day in a mental hospital.)

The Lady in Black continues to appear despite the fact that her remains and those of her husband have been removed to Georgia and despite the fact that

Fort Warren is today an historic site and tourist attraction. She is not seen weekly, monthly, or even
annually, as one might suspect, on the anniversary of
the hanging.

When will she next walk, the Lady in Black? No
one can say. Next week, perhaps, she will stroll the
battlements, a slender silhouette suffused with spectral light.

Then again, she may walk tonight.

The Mysterious Ticonderoga Curse

On a black, wind-screeching night two hundred years ago, Major Duncan Campbell of the Black Watch sat in his castle in the Scottish Highlands, warming himself by the fire.

How rackety the wind, welling up out of the moors. It set the leaded casements aclatter, screaked about the stone battlements and wheezed through the drafty corridors. Suddenly there was another sound, staccato in the wind, a pounding at the door so desperate that Duncan Campbell rose, almost in reflex, to answer it without waiting for one of the servants to do so.

There in his doorway tottered a wild-eyed highlander, his kilt splattered with blood. Fresh blood, not yet dry.

"Shield me," the stranger begged Duncan Campbell. "I have spilled blood this night and am being pursued. For God's sake, swear on your dirk to shield me." On impulse, Duncan Campbell drew his dagger and swore upon it to harbor the highlander.

His word given, he led the stranger down winding stone steps into the cellar, then into a far, all-but-hidden passageway. There, he knew, the man would be safe.

Duncan Campbell then returned to the great hall and the hearth. But no sooner had he settled into his chair than another thundering came at his door — many fists this time, battering with anger and excitement.

It was the search party.

"Donald Campbell has been murdered," they cried. "The murdering scoundrel fled this way. Have ye seen him, Duncan Campbell?"

His own cousin slain by the man he was concealing! What could he say? He had taken a solemn pledge to protect the man and a Campbell did not break his pledge.

No. He shook his head. No, he hadn't seen the murdering scoundrel. So the party was off.

Duncan Campbell did not sleep that night. Hour after hour he squirmed on his couch in the great room, trying to piece together what to do. Campbell blood stained the tartan of the man hiding in the cellar. Yet he had given the Campbell oath to protect the man who had spilled Campbell blood.

Suddenly there appeared in the gloom an apparition, shimmering, phantasmal. It was Donald Campbell, back from the dead.

"Inverawe! Inverawe!" his sepulchral voice intoned. (Inveraray was the seat of the Campbell clan.) "Blood has been shed! Shield not the murderer!" Then, as abruptly as it had materialized, the figure of Donald Campbell dissolved into silvery mist.

Next day, Duncan Campbell went straightaway to the murderer and told him of his dead cousin's ghostly visit.

"Aye," said the murderer. "That may well be. But you, Duncan Campbell, swore on your dirk to shield me."

Yes, it was true. Then suddenly it occurred to Duncan Campbell what he could do. On his lands the great mountain Ben Cruachan rose up, a stone behemoth brooding above the moors. It was a mountain by which the Campbell clan pledged its word. If he led the murderer there, Duncan Campbell reasoned, harbored him there, he would not be revoking his pledge. Still, he would have led the murderer from the shelter of his own roof. If the murderer escaped, that was the murderer's affair. He, Duncan Campbell, would have kept his word by providing him a place to hide.

That night Duncan Campbell led the assassin across the moors, up the craggy face of Ben Cruachan to a secret cave. The entrance was well buried in heather.

"You will be safe here," Duncan Campbell told the murderer, once they were inside. "It is a cave known to me only."

With the murderer out of his house, Duncan Campbell expected to rest peacefully that night. But he did not. The mountain Ben Cruachan was a place sacred to the Campbells. Was harboring the murderer of a Campbell there any less a crime than hiding him inside the Campbell castle?

As if to answer the question, the specter of Donald Campbell returned, suffused as before in eerie light.

"Inverawe! Inverawe!" the same ghostly voice rasped. "Blood has been shed! Shield not the murderer."

Early the next morning, Duncan Campbell made his way across the moors and up the slopes of Ben Cruachan to the cave. The fugitive had fled.

The matter was out of his hands now. And he, at last, could no longer be accused of shielding his cousin's murderer.

Duncan Campbell slept deeply that night. But not for long. A flash of light blazed through the room, yanking him up from sleep.

Once again his dead cousin stood before him.

"Farewell, Duncan Campbell," the ghost said, shaking his head reproachfully. "Farewell till we meet at Ticonderoga." Slowly, eerily, the specter receded into the darkness until only his face, solemn and foreboding, seemed to float upon the air.

"Farewell till we meet at Ticonderoga . . . " the disembodied head repeated, this time in a whisper barely audible.

A chill seized Duncan Campbell.

"Ticonderoga?" he said aloud. But there was no answer. The head had vanished. Then, slowly, carefully, Duncan Campbell mouthed the syllables . . . "Ti-con-der-o-ga . . ."

What place was that? A strange, foreign-sounding name it was. One he had never heard.

Several weeks later he was to hear it again.

It was the mid-1700s, time of the French and Indian War, and British troops, among them Scotland's Black Watch, were being dispatched to America to defeat the French in the Colonies.

Major Duncan Campbell found himself aboard ship nearing the New World. As they sailed into New York harbor and began moving up the Hudson River past the Palisades, past Hook Mountain and Bear Mountain, he learned from a fellow officer their mission. And their destination.

They were to attack first at Louisburg, then at Crown Point and finally — at Ticonderoga, the French-held fort at the head of Lake George.

Ticonderoga! His dead cousin's words came rushing back . . . "Farewell, Duncan Campbell. Farewell till we meet at Ticonderoga."

For the first time Duncan Campbell understood the meaning of the message from the other side of the grave. It was, in effect, his death sentence. He would fall at Ticonderoga.

The night before the attack on Fort Ticonderoga,

the ghost of Donald Campbell stood once again before Duncan Campbell, luminous, ominous.

"Farewell, Duncan Campbell," the apparition said as it had before. But then the words changed. "We *have met* at Ticonderoga."

"Have met . . . " Duncan Campbell repeated, knowing his fate was sealed.

As it turns out, Duncan Campbell did not die at Ticonderoga. But he was wounded along with thousands of British soldiers during Colonel Abercrombie's bungling attempt to capture Fort Ticonderoga from General Montcalm and the French. More than six thousand British soldiers and nine thousand provincials stormed Ticonderoga, and although they far outnumbered the French they were no match for them. The French had built an immense stockade of trees around the fort's outer walls so that Ticonderoga was virtually impregnable. And Abercrombie, stubbornly ordering his troops on, lost nearly half of them.

Duncan Campbell's wound — a piece of shrapnel in the arm — did not appear serious at the time. He was taken to the home of cousins, the Gilchrists, at nearby Fort Edward to recuperate. But gangrene set in and within two weeks Duncan Campbell was dead.

He was buried in the Gilchrist family plot, then reinterred a hundred years later at nearby Union Cemetery. Unlike others of his regiment who fell at

Ticonderoga, Major Duncan Campbell never made the final journey home to the Highlands (because of the "Campbell curse," it's said). He lies yet in the shadow of Ticonderoga, his grave marked by a simple stone:

> Here Lyes the Body of
> Duncan Campbell, of Invera-
> ray, Esq. Major to the old High-
> land Regiment, Aged 55 Years,
> who Died on the 17th of July,
> 1758, of the wounds received
> in the attack upon the Retrench-
> ments of Ticonderoga or Caril-
> lon on July 3, 1758.

The ghost of Donald Campbell walks no more. His murder has been avenged. But the story lingers on. In legend. In literature, in Robert Louis Stevenson's *The Master of Ballantrae*.

The Most Haunted House

One ghost per house would seem sufficient. But Woodburn, the Governor's Mansion in Dover, Delaware, claims not one . . . not two . . . not three . . . but *four* (and some say even more) different ghosts, as motley an assortment of specters as ever gathered under one roof.

To the casual stroller, Woodburn does not appear foreboding or sinister. It's an old house, true. Historic too, having been built in 1790 by John Hillyard on a tract of land given his great-grandfather by William Penn. It's a stately, uncluttered house, clean of line and, according to architectural historians, one of the finest examples of Federal architecture standing in America today. There's a sturdy, serene look about Woodburn — mauve, weather-mellowed bricks, large white-shuttered windows, a graceful fanlight. Moreover, nestling as it does amid towering pines, crepe myrtles and trim English boxwoods, Woodburn possesses a peacefulness characteristic of earlier, easier life-styles. Woodburn is, in fact, a peaceful, happy house. *Most* of the time.

But every now and then, for no accountable reason, one of its ghosts will become restive and go skulking through the shadows, or banging around in the dark, or shrieking above the wind. The four never consort . . . at least, they haven't to date.

Woodburn's ghostly antics have been going on for nearly two hundred years — *long* before the house became the official Governor's Mansion. The ghost stories were famous — good conversation pieces oft repeated. Yet no one in the General Assembly took them seriously in 1966 when it came time to appropriate funds for the purchase and renovation of Woodburn as Delaware's first official executive mansion.

So, the Governor's Mansion it became. And what of Delaware's first families who have lived there? Have they been terrorized by bumps in the night? Wraiths materializing out of thin air? Bone-numbing wails?

The late Charles L. Terry, Jr., the first Governor to occupy Delaware's "new" executive mansion, used to enjoy talking about the "tippling ghost," the "wino" who drained the cellar of some of its rarer vintages.

Earlier owners of the house, Terry liked to say, routinely filled decanters for the ghost who, without fail, would have emptied them by morning. One servant, according to Terry, swears he actually saw the ghost sitting in the dining room slowly sipping wine.

An old man he was, in powdered wig and Colonial dress.

The last of Woodburn's private owners, Dr. Frank Hall, also encountered the phantom wine fancier — or at least evidence of his presence. On more than one occasion, Dr. Hall discovered a bottle of wine "mysteriously" empty. The ghost into his cups again? Dr. Hall liked to think so.

This particular ghost was not the first to appear at Woodburn. That distinction belongs to an old-timer nicknamed the "Colonel." He appeared first in 1805 when Woodburn was occupied by a Dr. and Mrs. Bates. It was not the Bateses who encountered the "Colonel" but Lorenzo Dow, an itinerant Methodist evangelist who was staying at Woodburn while holding a series of revivals in Dover.

Going down to breakfast one morning, Dow passed in the upstairs hall a courtly but mysterious old gentleman, mysterious because Dow, in his days at Woodburn, had never seen him before. Dow smiled at the stranger, assuming him to be a newly arrived relative or guest, then thought nothing more of the incident until he joined the others at the breakfast table. When asked to lead the family in saying grace, Dow replied:

"But shouldn't we wait for the gentleman upstairs?"

Silence all around. And startled looks. Then Mrs. Bates answered crisply.

"There is no other guest in this house."

Dow was never invited back to Woodburn. But before he left, Mrs. Bates confided to him that she, too, had seen the old gentleman, that he was the "spitting image" of her father who had died at Woodburn. Another theory about the "Colonel" is that he is the ghost of a Revolutionary War colonel who died at Woodburn during the period that the house had served as a veterans' hospital shortly after the war.

Woodburn's other two ghosts? The noisiest one, a macabre chain rattler, is said to be the ghost of a slave kidnapper who was hung during a raid on Woodburn. (A busy stop on the Underground Railroad before the Civil War, the house was one of the secret way stations set up to harbor runaway slaves on their journeys north to freedom.) The clanging of chains is not heard inside the house so much as outside, welling up out of the hollow of an ancient tulip poplar (did the kidnapper swing from its branches?). There are blood-freezing moans, too, on nights when the wind is high and the moon is bright. The moans of many spirits, it's said, the cries of slaves who were captured or killed at Woodburn.

The fourth ghost? She is the gentlest of all, a wistful little girl wearing an old-fashioned, red-checked gingham dress. Who she is, where she came from, why she came to Woodburn all remain a mystery. As far as is known, she has materialized only once

— in the 1940s — to play by the pool in the garden. Unlike Woodburn's other ghosts, she appears to have had no place in the history of the house.

One day, perhaps, she will return. And make known her identity. Meanwhile, there are ghosts enough at Woodburn to lure the curious and the psychic. And to bemuse (and bedevil?) the first families who live there.

Abraham Lincoln, a Mourning Figure, Walks

No American house harbors more illustrious ghosts than the White House. Dolly Madison periodically flounces through the Rose Garden to make certain the gardeners tend it well; she planted the garden a hundred and fifty years ago and appeared in a fit of pique when the second Mrs. Woodrow Wilson ordered it dug up. Abigail Adams strings up the family wash in the East Room, William Henry Harrison pokes about the attic, Mrs. Grover Cleveland cries out in the night (she was the first First Lady to have a baby in the White House).

Some White House staffers tell of eerie encounters in the Rose Room, where Andrew Jackson's bed stands — unexplained chills, laughter cackling out of the bed. Others insist they have seen a fleeting ghost-child in the corridors. Little Willie Lincoln? Perhaps. He died in the White House at the age of twelve.

But the most celebrated White House ghost, indis-

putably, is that of Willie's father, Abraham Lincoln.

Grace Coolidge saw him first, a silhouette at a
window of the Oval Room, staring across the Poto-
mac Flats into Virginia, although for years White
House personnel had been attributing to Lincoln the
ghostly footsteps heard along the second-floor corridor. This pacing, and a knock at the door, roused
Queen Wilhelmina of the Netherlands one night
while she was visiting the Franklin D. Roosevelts.
She answered the knock, gasped, then fainted dead
away. There stood Abraham Lincoln, all six feet
four inches, in frock coat and top hat. Had she
dreamed it? Possibly; yet when she awoke, she was
lying on the floor.

When Queen Wilhelmina told President Roosevelt what had happened, he showed little surprise.
The Queen's bedroom was the Lincoln Room, he
explained, adding that Mrs. Roosevelt had also been
awakened by footsteps.

Mrs. Roosevelt, it is said, often felt Lincoln's presence in the White House, particularly late at night
while she was working on her papers. And just as
often little Fala, the President's Scottie, would ex-
plode into fits of barking for no apparent reason.

Once, one of Roosevelts' secretaries burst trembling from the Lincoln Room, crying that Lincoln
was there, sitting on the bed pulling off his boots. At
about the same time, a famous White House guest,
whose name has been kept secret, swears that while

she was sleeping in Lincoln's bed he tried to set fire to the mattress. That lady packed up and left, preferring an unhaunted Washington hotel to the White House.

Another person to sense Lincoln's nearness was his biographer, Carl Sandburg, who felt (but did not see) Lincoln join him by a window in the Oval Room. It was the window where Mrs. Coolidge had seen the silhouette and the window at which Lincoln himself had so often stood when troubled or perplexed.

"He was looking down, yet seeing nothing," wrote Army Chaplain E. C. Bolles, who had come one night to meet with Lincoln and been moved by the sight of him at the window in the Oval Room. "I think I never saw so sad a face in my life, and I have looked into many a mourner's face."

People who knew Lincoln remarked about his melancholy, his preoccupation, his near mystic quality. Was Lincoln psychic? Some parapsychologists believe so. It is true, for example, that Lincoln attended seances in the White House. True, too, that he had dabbled with spiritualism in his days as a young Illinois politician, that he turned to it more seriously after his son Willie died. Most historians deny, however, that Lincoln himself was a believer, maintaining that he agreed to the seances simply to please Mrs. Lincoln.

Maybe. But if so, why this letter written in 1842 to his good friend Joshua F. Speed? "I always did

have a strong tendency to mysticism . . . I have had
so many evidences of God's direction, so many in-
stances when I have been controlled by some other
power than my own will that I cannot doubt that
this power comes from above."

Even the most skeptical historians admit that Lincoln believed his dreams to be prophetic. Once,
while Mrs. Lincoln was visiting in Philadelphia with
their son Tad, Lincoln telegraphed her from the
White House:

PUT TAD'S PISTOL AWAY
I HAD AN UGLY DREAM ABOUT HIM

Lincoln also dreamed of his own assassination ten days
before it happened.

> I retired late, he wrote. I soon began to
> dream. There seemed to be a deathlike still-
> ness about me. Then I heard subdued sobs, as
> if a number of people were weeping.
> I thought I left my bed and wandered down-
> stairs. There the silence was broken by the
> same pitiful sobbing, but the mourners were
> invisible. I went from room to room; no liv-
> ing person was in sight, but the same mourn-
> ful sounds of distress met me as I passed
> along.
> It was light in all the rooms; every object
> was familiar to me; but where were all the
> people who were grieving as if their hearts

would break? I was puzzled and alarmed. What could be the meaning of all this? Determined to find the cause of a state of things so mysterious and so shocking, I kept on until I arrived at the East Room, which I entered. Before me was a catafalque, on which rested a corpse wrapped in funeral vestments. Around it were stationed soldiers who were acting as guards; and there was a throng of people, some gazing mournfully upon the corpse, whose face was covered, others weeping pitifully. "Who is dead in the White House?" I demanded of one of the soldiers. "The President," was his answer. "He was killed by an assassin." Then came a loud burst of grief from the crowd, which awoke me from my dream. I slept no more that night; and although it was only a dream, I have been strangely annoyed by it ever since.

On the night before the assassination, Lincoln had another dream so troubling he related it at a cabinet meeting the following morning.

"I had a warning dream again last night," he began. "It related to water. I seemed to be in a singular and indescribable vessel that was moving with great rapidity toward a dark and indefinite shore."

That same day Lincoln told his bodyguard, W. H. Crook, that he had dreamed for three nights running that he would be assassinated. Crook begged the

President not to go to the theater, but Lincoln said that he must go, that he had promised Mrs. Lincoln.

Later, when leaving for the theater, Lincoln said not "Good night" to Crook, as had been his habit, but "Good-bye."

Afterward, in his memoirs, Crook wrote that he believed the President knew he would meet his fate at the theater.

But to return to Lincoln's ghost. It has not been seen or heard lately — why, no one knows although some say it vanished while the White House was being renovated during the Truman administration.

Truman, certainly, seems to be the last President to have commented — publicly, at least — about Lincoln's ghost. And he did so in jest, explaining to a visitor that the thumps and bumps he had heard in the night "must have been Abe."

There is, however, a second Lincoln ghost, a phantom funeral train seen every April somewhere along the route of the official funeral train. So graphic were the descriptions of the New York Central yardmen at Albany that the *Evening Times* printed this account:

> Regularly in the month of April, about midnight the air on the tracks becomes very keen and cutting. On either side of the tracks it is warm and still. Every watchman, when he feels the air, slips off the track and sits down

to watch. Soon the pilot engine of Lincoln's funeral train passes with long, black streamers and with a band of black instruments playing dirges, grinning skeletons sitting all about.

It passes noiselessly. If it is moonlight, clouds come over the moon as the phantom train goes by. After the pilot engine passes, the funeral train itself with flags and streamers rushes past. The track seems covered with black carpet, and the coffin is seen in the center of the car, while all about it in the air and on the train behind are vast numbers of blue-coated men, some with coffins on their backs, others leaning upon them.

If a real train were passing its noise would be hushed as if the phantom train rode over it. Clocks and watches always stop as the phantom train goes by and when looked at are five to eight minutes behind.

Everywhere on the road about April 27 watches and clocks are suddenly found to be behind.

Are there other Lincoln apparitions? There may be. Mediums both here and abroad periodically report being in communication with Lincoln. And, ever since his burial in Springfield, Illinois, more than a hundred years ago, talk persists of strange doings at the grave site (some believe the grave is empty) and of endless footsteps in the night.

It is portentous, and a thing of state
That here at midnight, in our little town,
A mourning figure walks, and will not rest,
Near the old court-house pacing up and down.

Vachel Lindsay,

"Abraham Lincoln Walks at Midnight
(in Springfield, Illinois)"

Virginia's Ghostly Aristocrat

S*he comes* *not* to haunt or harass. Not to spite or avenge. Her only wish, it's said, is to come home again. Home to Westover on the James River where she was born in 1707. Home to the boxwood gardens where she romped as a child, to the green velvet lawns she wandered as a young girl, to the proud, tall-chimneyed plantation house where she died, at not quite thirty, of a broken heart.

She is Evelyn Byrd, daughter of William Byrd II, agent of the colony of Virginia to King George I, founder of the capital city of Richmond, surveyor of the dividing line between Virginia and North Carolina. She is also of that First Family of Virginians that claims Antarctic explorer Admiral Richard E. Byrd and Senator Harry F. Byrd.

Today, almost two hundred and fifty years after her death, Evelyn Byrd continues to appear at Westover although the estate, thanks to her half brother's excesses, had to be sold after the Revolutionary War to pay his debts. Evelyn's visits are infrequent and

unpredictable. But never alarming. She crosses from
another age, another world, yet, strangely, she materializes not as an eerie, spectral being from the Beyond. She comes gently, smilingly.

There is warmth in her smile. Tenderness. And
therein lies a mystery.

Why the happy return to a place where life had
been so empty, lonely, and unbearable that she was
dead at twenty-nine of no diagnosable malady?

Evelyn's early years at Westover may have been
happy. (Certainly they were pampered. She was so
much her daddy's girl that when, at the age of two,
she wet her bed, it was her nurse, not she, who was
punished.) But Evelyn's early years at Westover
were short. She was shipped to England at the age of
ten to be educated, and returned nine years later, a
beautiful young lady suffering from a broken romance. During the last eleven years of her life, Westover became a sort of prison. A gilded cage where
Evelyn withered away, yearning for the "unsuitable"
English Baronet her father had forbidden her to
marry.

It all began in London during the summer of Evelyn's sixteenth year. She had had a brilliant season;
had been painted by Charles Bridges wearing a low-
cut green gown that emphasized her gardenia-petal
skin, chestnut hair and exotic, slanting, blue-green
eyes; had been presented to King George I, who was
so enamored of her dash and elegance that he ex-

claimed, "Are there any other as beautiful birds in my forests of America?"

That same summer Evelyn fell recklessly in love with a nobleman she had met at court — who, exactly, remains a secret. Some historians believe he was Charles Morduant, the grandson of Lord Peterborough. Others suspect Evelyn's lover was Lord Peterborough, himself, a man four times her age, a man Thackeray characterized in *Henry Esmond* as "that noble old madcap." Whoever Evelyn's lover, he was wholly unsuitable by Byrd's standards. Not a man to sit idly by, Byrd dashed off threatening letters to both Evelyn and her lover. He wrote to Evelyn:

> To *Amasia* ("the beloved one")
>
> Considering ye solemn promise you made me, first by word of mouth & afterward by letter, that you wou'd not from thence forth have any Converse or Correspondence with the Baronet, I am astonisht you have violated that protestation in a most notorious manner. The gracious audience you gave him the morning you left ye Towne & the open conversations you have with him in the Country have been too unguarded to be denied. Tis therefor high time for me to reproach you with breech of duty & breech of faith and once more to repeat to you my strict and positive Commands never more to see, to speak or write to

that Gentleman or to give him an opportunity to see, speak or write to You. I also forbid you to enter into any promise or engagement with him of marriage or Inclination . . . And that neither he nor you may be deluded afterwards with Vain hopes of forgiveness; I have put it out of my power by vowing that I never will. And as to any Expectation you may fondly entertain of a Fortune from me, you are not to look for one brass farthing . . . Nay besides all that I will avoid the sight of you as of a creature detested.

Figure then to yourself, my Dear Child, how wretched you will be with a provokt father and a disappointed Husband. To whome then will you fly in your distress . . . ? For God's sake then, my dear child, for my sake & your own, survey the desperate Precipice you stand upon, and don't rashly cast yourself down head long into Ruin. The idle Promises this man makes you will all vanish into smoke, & instead of Love he will slight & abuse you when he finds his hopes of Fortune disappointed. Then you & your children (if you should be so miserable to have any) must be Beggars, & you may be assur'd all the world will deservedly despise you, & you will hardly be pity'd so much as by Him who would fain continue, &c . . .

To Evelyn's lover he wrote:

> To *Erranti* ("knight errant")
>
> What success these worthy steps have met
> with in the Girle I know not; but they shall
> never meet with any in the Father. I fear
> your circumstances are not flourishing
> enough to maintain a wife in much splendour
> . . . I have made my will since I heard of
> your good intentions toward me, & have be-
> queathed my Daughter a splendid shilling if
> she marrys any man that tempts her to disobe-
> dience. After giving you this friendly warn-
> ing, I hope you will have discretion enough
> to leave off so unprofitable a Pursuit, to
> which no tears on my Daughter's part, or In-
> treatys on yours will ever be able to recon-
> cile . . .

The affair was ended. The Baronet, as far as is
known, made no further attempts to see Evelyn. She
continued the social life in court circles but with a
sadness ill-suited to her youth and loveliness.

Less than three years later — in 1726 — Evelyn,
her younger sister Wilhelmina, her father and new
stepmother (her own mother had died some years
earlier in London of smallpox) sailed for Virginia and
Westover.

Evelyn readjusted poorly, withdrawing more and
more into herself. There were beaus in the begin-

ning, but none, evidently, to Evelyn's liking. Byrd
was concerned:

"One of the most Antick Virgins I am acquainted
with," he wrote England's Earl of Orrery, "is my
daughter. Either our Fellows are not smart eno' for
her, or she seems too smart for them, but in a little
Time I hope they will split the difference . . ."

They never did "split the difference" and in the
final years of her young life Evelyn became a recluse,
seeing only her dear friend Anne Carter, who had recently married Benjamin Harrison of neighboring
Berkeley Plantation. The two girls met nearly every
afternoon — to embroider, to talk, to dream — either
at Westover or Berkeley or, if the afternoons were
warm and sunny, in the cool poplar grove adjoining
the two plantations.

Did Evelyn suspect her days were numbered?
Perhaps. She and Anne had made a pact: the first to
die would try to return, but "in such a fashion not to
frighten anyone."

Appropriately, Anne Harrison was the first to see
Evelyn's ghost. But the confrontation came some
months after Evelyn had been buried in the small
cemetery just west of Westover. Disconsolate over
her friend's death, Anne refused at first to revisit the
poplar grove. For fear that Evelyn would not be
there? Or that she *would* be? Ghostly and forbidding?

Finally Anne did go. And as she strolled underneath the tulip trees where the two had spent so many hours, shared so many confidences, she felt "a presence." She turned and saw an "ethereal figure" approaching. It was Evelyn. She greeted Anne with a smile, then vanished.

It has been thus ever since — a quick, smiling appearance — whenever, wherever Evelyn has materialized. She always comes gently, felicitously, "in such a fashion not to frighten anyone." Often she is mistaken for a family member, a friend, a houseguest at Westover because she seems so very real, "so very flesh-and-blood."

Sometimes she wears green velvet and lace. But more often she is dressed simply in white. She may appear in one of the corridors at Westover — as if on an errand. She has been seen on the back stair to the pantry, in a passage under the main mahogany stair that sweeps three stories up through the center of the house, in the southeast bedroom, which had been her room (a workman once saw her there, preening before the mirror).

Evelyn's favorite haunts, however, are the gardens, the grounds, and the poplar grove between Westover and Berkeley. Once she was seen strolling in the company of another young girl. Anne Harrison?

Ghosts, it is said, return to the world of the living because of "unfinished business." Of missions unaccomplished, messages undelivered, scores unsettled. Is Evelyn Byrd's business to announce that she has been reunited with her English lover? That she has found in death the happiness she had been denied in life?

Romantics would have it thus.

The Silver Doe

On dark and moonless nights, a silver-white doe races through the gnarled forests of Roanoke Island, North Carolina. No bullet or arrow can harm her. No rope can hold her.

She is a ghost.

The ghost of Virginia Dare, some say. She is bewitched, doomed forever to roam her lonely island, searching for her people who vanished mysteriously nearly four hundred years ago.

Virginia Dare was the first English child born in Colonial America. Her people were sent to the New World by Sir Walter Raleigh to found a colony. They arrived in 1587 and that same year Virginia was born. She was a beautiful child with hair the color of sunshine and eyes the deep blue of the ocean. A fairy princess, it seemed. A good omen.

But such was not the case. The colonists' crops failed. Food ran low. Without provisions, the English could not last the winter. So Captain John White, the colony's governor and Virginia's grand-

father, sailed to England for food, promising to return as soon as his ship was loaded. He left nine days after Virginia was born.

There are some who say that as soon as Captain White sailed, Chief Wanchese, leader of a hostile tribe of Indians, led an attack on Fort Raleigh. They say if it had not been for Wanchese's neighbor and rival, the friendly Chief Manteo, all would have died. Because Manteo knew of a secret tunnel linking the fort to the sea, he was able to save the baby Virginia and her mother. Virginia's father might have survived, too, if he had not stopped to carve a fatal message on a tree.

When Captain White returned from England four years later, he found Fort Raleigh in ruins and his kinsmen gone. There wasn't a clue except for three letters — C R O — carved into the trunk of a tree.

How could an entire colony vanish without a trace? What did C R O mean? Had the colonists crossed Croatan Sound in search of food? Had they joined the Croatan Indians? Or had they been massacred by them?

Captain White never learned the fate of his people. And to this day no one knows what became of the "Lost Colony."

Legend says Manteo's people welcomed Virginia and her mother, making them blood sisters. Each year Virginia seemed to become more beautiful. Two of the tribe fell desperately in love with her

— a handsome young brave named Okisko and Chico, the Medicine Man.

Okisko was content to wait, hoping that Virginia's friendship might turn into love. But Chico was impatient. Each time Virginia smiled at Okisko, Chico seethed with jealousy. When Virginia turned down Chico's proposal of marriage, he flew into a rage, vowing that she would never marry anyone — and most definitely not Okisko.

Being a medicine man, Chico could cast spells and bewitch people. He knew, says the legend, that the pied purple pearls of mussels could be used for black magic. Trapped inside each pearl was a water nymph who, once freed, would obey any command. Chico began collecting the evil pearls, and when he had enough for a necklace he strung them together.

Next he built a giant canoe mounted with sails like those on the ship that had brought Virginia's people to the New World. By promising to lead Virginia to her people, he lured her aboard, then sped across the sound. As they neared Roanoke Island, Chico brought forth the magic necklace.

Virginia had never seen anything so dazzling. Innocently she fastened it around her neck. The fire of the pearls glowed in Chico's eyes. His plan was working. Virginia was in his power.

When they arrived at Roanoke Island, Virginia splashed through the surf onto the beach. She fell to her knees. Something strange was happening. She could not move. Her hands and feet throbbed dreadfully. Then she saw that they were turning into hooves.

In an instant it was over. There was no Virginia. There was only a silver doe fleeing into the woods, and a single human footprint in the sand.

No one in Manteo's village had seen Chico and Virginia leave. So no one could explain Virginia's sudden disappearance. Chico went about his business, pretending to be as baffled as the others. Soon, however, tales reached the tribe about the silver doe on Roanoke Island. Okisko began to suspect foul play.

The silver doe, he decided, was Virginia. Rather than consult Chico, whom he distrusted, Okisko sought out an old friend in a nearby village who was also a medicine man.

If the silver doe was Virginia, could she be made human again? The medicine man said that she could and told Okisko what he must do.

First, he must bathe in the magic fountain that bubbled up in the center of Roanoke Island. Next he must make an enchanted arrow that could pierce the doe's heart without killing her. For the point of the arrow he must find the eyetooth of a shark, for its shaft a green witchhazel stick, and for the plume a feather from the wing of a great blue heron.

All of this Okisko did. Then he thrust the arrow deep into the magic fountain, as he also had been instructed, and left it there three days and nights. On the fourth day at dawn, Okisko seized the magic arrow and set out to hunt the silver doe.

What he did not know, however, was that his tribe's old rival, Chief Wanchese, was out hunting that same morning. His quarry, too, was the silver doe.

Okisko and Wanchese spied the doe at the same instant. Both arrows flew. Okisko's was first to hit its mark. The doe dissolved in a silver mist, and out stepped Virginia, only to be felled an instant later by Wanchese's arrow.

Okisko scooped up Virginia and raced to the magic fountain. To his dismay, when he bathed her in the crystal waters, the fountain dried up and Virginia vanished before his eyes. In place of the fountain a vine sprang forth, laden with grapes that were the blue of Virginia's eyes.

Heartsick, Okisko turned to go. As he did so, he caught sight of a silver doe retreating into the wood.

As long as he lived, Okisko stalked the silver doe, hoping one day Virginia would resume her human form.

She never did. But to this day the silver doe roams Roanoke Island, her silhouette luminous against the forests of live oak. And old-timers swear that she is most often seen gazing at the grassy ramparts of Fort Raleigh from which Virginia's people vanished nearly four hundred years ago.

The Gray Man

They say that only those with second sight see the Gray Man of Pawleys Island, South Carolina. Or those "born with the caul." Or seventh daughters of seventh daughters — all persons able to communicate with those on the other side of death.

They sometimes see him emerging from the surf, wrapped in the mists of early morning. Or they see him at midnight in a cutaway suit and turtleshell-shaped hat, motionless atop a dune, gazing seaward. Or they see him in the first dark of day, lounging on the second story piazza of the old Pelican Inn. They may even see him at midday, wandering the beach like dozens of other swimmers and sunbathers.

He looks at first, swear those who have seen him on the beach, like anyone else. A little thin, perhaps. A bit short. But as he nears, then passes, they realize with a shudder that he is faceless. That he has no eyes, no nose and no mouth. They know then that they have seen the Gray Man, that if they should turn and look back, he will be gone. They know,

too, that if they value their lives, they must be gone. As quickly as possible. The Gray Man has warned them, as he has warned others, that a hurricane is coming.

It has always been thus. At least as long as Pawleys old-timers can recollect. They do not take the Gray Man's appearances lightly because disaster inevitably gallops in on his heels. Those who scoff are apt to do so only once — either they're swept to their reward by a hurricane's fury or so nearly so that if they manage somehow to ride out the storm they are sobered by the experience and henceforth show respect for the Gray Man. "Respect" is the proper word because the Gray Man comes to alert rather than to alarm, to give islanders enough advance warning to batten down and make for the safety of the mainland.

Who is the Gray Man? Where does he come from? Why does he come? And why to Pawleys Island only? Why not to Myrtle Beach farther north on South Carolina's Grand Strand where there are twenty, perhaps thirty times as many people? Why not to Windy Hill or Crescent Beach or Cherry Grove where hurricanes can also strike awesome blows?

Some believe the Gray Man is the spirit of old Percival Pawley who settled first on the island, gave it his name, and loved it so that he refuses to leave, even in death. Others insist that the Gray Man is the star-crossed lover of a famous Charleston belle. And that is the story most people tell. It begins about two hundred years ago.

The families of the two lovers — both "Old Charleston," proud and powerful — were against the match from the start. First of all, the lovers were cousins. "Blood cousins," as they say in the South. Cousins, in that day, did marry cousins, mostly to keep family bloodlines pure. But in this case, both families were adamant that there be no marriage. The young man, all of Charleston knew and his own family readily admitted, was a malcontent and ne'er-do-well. The girl could not have been more opposite. She had beauty of the legendary sort, she was musical, artistic, well read and articulate. Moreover, she was gracious and gentle. And she was besieged by beaus far worthier than her cousin.

It was her cousin, however, that she had chosen. In the beginning, the parents more or less ignored the romance, believing that it would flare up and then die. But it didn't. The couple's love for one another deepened and intensified. Just when it seemed there was no way to break up the match, the parents met to seek a solution. The young man, they decided, must be sent to Europe where he would meet new friends and, with luck, find new love. As for the girl, she would forget and, the parents believed, eventually forgive.

The young man put up almost no resistance

(proof, the parents believed, that a marriage would have been disastrous) and sailed away to France. He promised to return, to remain true, but within a few months word came that he had been killed in a duel, fought over the hand of a famous French beauty.

His fiancée was shattered. She withdrew from family and friends, closeted herself in her room, ate little and slept less. She seemed bewitched, removed altogether from reality. No one could reach her.

And then one day an old friend came to call, a handsome young man who had recently lost his wife. His grief, the girl realized, was surely as intense as her own. So she saw him. That day, and the next and the next. Their common bond — grief — turned to affection and before long, to love.

Within a few months, the two had married. They settled on a rice plantation north of Charleston and, like many Charlestonians, took a house at Pawleys Island for the "fever months," May to October, when heat hung over the Low Country like wet cotton and mosquitoes swirled up from the swamps, spreading malaria over the land. Pawleys Island, catching the wind off the sea, was cool and mosquitoless, a safe retreat.

In the summer of 1778, the young wife retreated to Pawleys Island as usual, but her husband, now a commander fighting the Revolution alongside Francis Marion, South Carolina's famous "Swamp Fox," was able to slip over to Pawleys perhaps one weekend out of six.

On a weekend when the wife was alone, a hurricane churned out of the South Atlantic and drove a brigantine to the bottom just offshore in front of Island House where she was staying. All hands were lost. Or so it was thought. But late that night, in the eerie calm that characteristically follows each hurricane, a lone survivor straggled ashore, made his way to Island House, knocked twice, then slumped against the door. He was brought in and when the young wife saw him, she collapsed.

It was her cousin, back from the dead.

The cousin, seeing the love he had betrayed, fled from Island House and from Pawleys Island. He was never seen again alive. Fever seized him shortly after he reached the mainland and he died within a few days.

The young wife recovered from the shock, was reunited with her husband and seemed to live happily ever after *except* when she visited Pawleys Island. There she was haunted by a shadowy figure skulking in the dunes. Was it her cousin? She believed so although she never knew. Only once did she see the figure close up and only then did she realize that his face was as gray and featureless as the sea.

In the beginning, it was she alone who saw the figure. But in time others began to see him, too, always before a hurricane, always in time to seek refuge on the mainland. Old-timers tell of how he appeared before the storms of 1822, 1893 and 1916, before Hurricane Hazel in 1954 and again the following year just before Connie flattened the Carolina coast. And they credit each of the Gray Man's appearances with saving thousands of lives. Is he the star-crossed lover, destined as penance to roam the dunes and beaches forevermore?

Whoever he is, this much is certain. He is as much a part of Pawleys Island as the dunes and beaches, relentlessly shifted and reshaped by the sea, the scarecrow oaks trailing tatters of Spanish moss, the laughing gulls squealing overhead as they ride the wind, the spray-weathered beach houses, crouching crablike in the dunes, the bones of old wrecks, alternately disinterred and buried by the tides. He belongs to Pawleys Island in an era of weather satellites and hurricane hunts as he did in the age of sail. His visits continue. And continue to be heeded.

The Harp Player of Pitcher's Point

On the Mississippi Gulf Coast, between Pass Christian and Long Beach, is a barren stretch of land known locally as Pitcher's Point. Some say the place got its name because the ragged coastline forms the shape of a pitcher there. Others say it was named for a pirate who put his curse on the spot in the 1700s. Still others say it's because nothing will grow there except marsh grass and pitcher plants.

But everyone agrees the spot is haunted — and that's why, despite the booming tourist trade, nobody is fool enough to build a fancy hotel or a seafood restaurant there. When someone did try, a few years ago, the place was promptly blown away by a hurricane. More than one old fisherman swore that above the scream of the high winds he could hear the faint, ghostly sound of a harp.

Once, over a hundred years ago, when "The Pass" was a famous winter resort, there was a house at Pitcher's Point — a large, elegant two-story mansion facing the Gulf. On summer evenings gay colored

lanterns could be seen swinging over its wide veran-
das while laughing belles in silken gowns danced
across it with their handsome partners.

The owner of the house, a rich and popular sea
captain, enjoyed giving parties; and the society of
Pass Christian was happy to accept his invitations.
Besides being charming and wealthy, the captain had
a certain air of mystery that appealed to all the ro-
mantic young ladies.

The captain's arrival at Pass Christian had been
highly dramatic — his ship, en route from South
America to New Orleans, had caught fire and burned
just offshore. All Pass Christian remembered that
terrible night: the blazing ship, the shrieks of the
trapped passengers, the hasty launching of small
boats, the futile search for survivors. Curiously, some
of the would-be rescuers reported that as they neared
the flaming hulk they heard the eerie strains of a
harp, and the voice of a woman singing. People on
shore thought they had heard the music, too.

The next morning, the ship's captain had been
found crawling on the beach, dazed and black with
soot. His first mate, a swarthy bearded fellow, was
lying unconscious nearby. Taken in by the towns-
people, the men gradually recovered, but the captain
obviously found it too painful to speak of the great
tragedy. He had done all he could to save the passengers, yet he blamed himself for the loss of life. If
it had not been for his faithful first mate, who had

somehow managed to drag him into a rowboat, he too would have perished.

Nobody blamed the captain, and they were pleased when he decided to settle in their community. Everyone admired the beautiful house he built overlooking the Gulf, and no one seemed to think it unusual that he paid for it with Spanish gold. For over a year the captain's popularity grew.

Then his first mate, who had become his servant, was stricken by a tropical fever. In his delirium, he began to moan aloud: "I have sinned . . . I must confess . . ."

Gradually, from words like "murder" and "gold" and "the lady with the harp," the local doctor who attended him pieced together the real story of what had happened the night the ship burned.

It seemed that among the ship's passengers there had been an enormously wealthy, but ugly old Brazilian and his beautiful young wife, the "lady with the harp," who played every night for the ship's company. But the lady was not happy. She yearned for romance, and the young captain was all too willing.

Soon she was playing love songs for him, and the captain was infatuated with her. His infatuation turned into an obsession when he learned that her ugly old husband had a trunk full of gold coins in his stateroom. One night when he caught the old Bra-

zilian on deck alone, he simply shoved him over-
board. An unfortunate accident, alas — a feeble,
crippled man on a slippery deck . . .

But the wife guessed. Overcome with remorse and
guilt, she begged the captain to confess his crime to a
priest, and swore she would never marry a murderer.
Now every night she played, not love songs for the
captain, but *Ave Marias* for her dead husband.

As the ship neared New Orleans, the captain
began to panic. Suppose his beautiful lady turned
him in to the authorities when they landed? Then he
would have neither lover nor gold.

It was at this point that he confided in his first
mate, and together they planned to set fire to the ship
close to a harbor on the Gulf Coast. In the general
confusion, they would have ample time to stow the
trunk of gold coins in a rowboat and get safely away.
Once ashore, they could bury the trunk in the sand
of deserted Pitcher's Point, returning to it later. . .

Of course, the doctor did not fit the story together
all at once, but every time he visited the dying first
mate, he became more suspicious, and learned a little
more.

One night, burning with fever, the little man cried
out piteously for the windows to be closed. "The
lady with the harp!" he raved. "She is playing now!
Ave Maria . . ." and he sank down on his pillow,
near death. The doctor felt a chill down his spine,

and looked up to see the captain standing in the doorway. Neither man spoke, and the first mate died that night.

The doctor was a cautious man, and after all was not quite sure how much to believe of the first mate's delirious tale. However, he did confide in a friend, and maybe that friend told another friend, for suddenly there were rumors rippling through Pass Christian about the mysterious sea captain. At his next party, certain important social leaders were conspicuously absent, and among those present there was a great deal of whispering. The doctor thought the captain looked strained and nervous. Would he panic, as according to the first mate he had panicked before? Surely he must be wondering just how much the doctor had learned or guessed.

After the party, the doctor and his friend waited in the shadows outside the captain's house. Soon the captain emerged, carrying a shovel and heading for the beach. They followed him down to the shore and watched from a distance as he began digging in the sand. Harder and harder he dug; then there was a scrape of metal on metal, and the captain dropped the shovel and sank to his knees. He was pulling at a dark bulky object.

But suddenly he lifted his head and looked out to sea. The doctor and his friend heard it, too — the weird, floating strains of a harp. As the two men watched, the ghostly outline of a rowboat appeared from the mist. At the oars sat four wraithlike figures, and standing slender and beautiful in the bow was a dark-haired young woman plucking a harp.

Then there was a hoarse cry from the shore, and the music abruptly ceased. The doctor wrenched his eyes away from the ghostly rowboat in time to see the captain lurch forward. He ran to him, but the man was dead, having apparently struck his temple on the open lid of the iron trunk. The trunk itself was empty, but clenched in the captain's hand were three gold coins.

When the doctor looked out to sea again, the boat and its crew had vanished, but he thought he could hear, faint on the wind, a ripple of melody.

Even today, when the wind is right, people swear you can hear the haunting harp music at Pitcher's Point, and occasionally, on foggy nights, fishermen report catching sight of a battered old rowboat with spectral oarsmen. But the real believers like to point out that the trouble started long before the Brazilian lady's harp music was first heard at Pitcher's Point, maybe a hundred years earlier, when a pirate put his curse on the spot.

If the star-crossed sea captain had chosen another place to burn up his ship and bury his treasure, he might have fared better.

Goat Castle

In the golden days of Natchez, Mississippi, there lived four glamorous young people who were the envy of all who watched them galloping about on their spirited horses, dancing at glittering balls, strolling through the camelia gardens of their antebellum mansions.

All four were rich, handsome, talented, aristocratic, and the very best of friends. Jennie Merrill, whose father owned Elmscourt Plantation, was an imperious little beauty who had been presented at the Court of St. James's while still in her teens. Her beau, Duncan Minor, was heir to a large fortune and considered the finest catch in Natchez. Brilliant and dashing Octavia Dockery wrote poetry and was headed for a literary career; sensitive Dick Dana, son of the Episcopal rector, had studied to be a concert pianist. For Jennie and Dunc, Octavia and Dick, the future looked promising indeed.

Yet all four were destined for tragedy — tragedy that brought poverty, scandal, madness, murder, and

a hatred that extended years beyond the grave. Probably no one will ever know the true story behind the mystery of Goat Castle, but parts of the puzzle can be fitted together . . .

Jennie's world began to crumble first. Her father died, and the family split up; Jennie went to live alone at Glenburnie, just across the road from her beloved childhood home. Next, her engagement to Dunc Minor was broken by Dunc's mother, who refused to permit the two to marry because they were cousins.

Embittered, Jennie withdrew from society and shut the gates of Glenburnie to everyone — except Dunc, who continued to live with his mother but rode out to see Jennie every night. People whispered that he stayed until dawn; there was speculation that the couple might be secretly married. But the situation affected Dunc; he became almost as antisocial as Jennie.

At Glenwood, just across a wooded thicket from Glenburnie, Octavia and Dick Dana, now married, were having troubles, too. Dick's dreams of a career as a concert pianist were shattered one terrible day when he started to lower a window and it crashed down, mutilating his fingers. Unable to accept this cruel trick of fate, Dick would sit for hours at his piano, missing notes, pretending not to hear the discords.

As Dick's inheritance dwindled, Octavia put aside

her poetry to clean the house and cook the meals. Eventually the Danas had to dismiss the last servant, and Octavia was forced to care for the livestock and work the farm herself. Dick couldn't or wouldn't help.

He was beginning to act irrationally. Some days he'd forget his own name. Other days he would play the piano as though possessed. He took to wandering in the woods, hiding behind trees whenever he saw someone coming. Once Octavia found him up in a tree, dressed in a potato sack. He brought home stray dogs, cats, ducks and goats, which he allowed to roam free through the house. As Dick and Octavia's life together crumbled, so, too, did the plantation house. One of the big columns collapsed and crashed onto the front porch; the upper gallery sagged. There was no money for repairs, and Octavia, exhausted with work and worry, crept about like a sharecropper's wife.

Proud and snobbish Jennie Merrill, living just across the woods at Glenburnie, couldn't bear such slovenly neighbors — although Dick and Octavia had once been dear friends. When their goats wandered across her manicured lawn and began nibbling at her roses and neatly pruned hedges, she snatched her gun and shot two of them — opening shots, it turned out, of a war between the two houses. Jennie tried to coerce Dunc to buy Glenwood, so that she could put Dick and Octavia out.

One hot summer afternoon, a shot rang out at Glenburnie. Negroes working in Miss Jennie's cotton fields heard screams . . . then more shots . . . then a low moaning in the woods. They did not investigate. (In that day it would not have been their place to do so.)

Dick and Octavia must surely have heard the shots and screams, too — yet they didn't go over to Glenburnie to see what was wrong. At dusk, when Dunc Minor rode up for his nightly visit, he discovered the house empty and the drawing room a shambles of blood-spattered, overturned furniture. There was no sign of Jennie.

It was the sheriff's men who found her — at dawn — clad in a blue cotton dress, barefoot — and dead. She was lying in the woods separating Glenburnie and Glenwood.

The murder caused a sensation in Natchez. And baffled the police. Who had killed Miss Jennie Merrill? Octavia, who had quarreled with her over the goats? Dick, who frequently wandered in the woods where her body was found? Dunc Minor, first at the scene of the crime, who stood to inherit her money? One of the plantation help? Or was the murderer a casual robber?

Clues tangled, crossed, led nowhere. A bloody overcoat left in the drawing room and smudged fingerprints made by a "deformed" hand seemed to point to Dick — but witnesses testified that they had heard him playing at the approximate time of the crime. (Dick and Octavia were charged with the murder, but later released.)

The crime was never solved.

For Dick and Octavia, life was never the same again. While they were in jail, curiosity-seekers invaded their house, then shrank in horror at what they saw. Dust lay inches thick on old rosewood furniture, a fine sofa had been chopped up for firewood, floors were littered with broken window glass, newspapers, feathers from tattered mattresses. Hens nested in priceless antique chairs, pigs rooted in the garbage-strewn kitchen, and goats wandered everywhere — up and down the staircases, munching on damask draperies, on satin upholstery, on rare first editions yanked from the bookshelves.

By the time Dick and Octavia were released from jail, Glenwood had been dubbed "Goat Castle."

For a time the two were famous. Tourists flocked to see Goat Castle; Octavia collected fifty cents a head and showed them around, carrying a goat in her arms, while Dick obligingly played the piano — the handsome grand that had somehow, mysteriously, escaped the general decay. For a while, the couple seemed grotesquely happy. But gradually the visitors stopped coming.

It was then that the stories started. People were afraid to walk past the thicket that separated Goat Castle from Glenburnie, because the woods were said to be haunted by Miss Jennie's unavenged ghost. Sometimes, late in the afternoons, you could see her flitting from tree to tree, barefoot, wearing her blue cotton dress. Other times, you could hear her moaning. Her wails grew louder and louder, until another sound welled up to overpower them — the crashing chords of Dick's piano.

Strangely, Dick's playing was never heard until dusk — about the time Miss Jennie's ghost was supposed to walk. People said Dick simply couldn't endure hearing her sad moans, that to drown them out he ripped into the keyboard. Strangest of all, the music he now played was powerful and passionate, *despite* his crippled hand. He no longer tinkled through the little waltzes he had played for the tourists at Goat Castle. He performed brilliantly — as though on a concert stage.

Years went by; Goat Castle decayed and crumbled; Octavia died. Finally, Dick himself died. Weeds have grown up, hiding the ruins of the old plantation house. But, natives of Natchez say, ghosts still haunt the place. Just before dark, you can hear a low, eerie moaning in the woods — and then, a moment later, the thunderous chords and rich arpeggios of a piano played by a master.

Marie Laveau, Queen of the Voodoos

Elmore Lee Banks won't easily forget the day he stopped in a drugstore in New Orleans' French Quarter for a cold soda. He was just about to order when the counterman started at something just beyond his shoulder, dropped his ice cream scoop, blanched and fled.

Elmore looked around and saw standing behind him an old woman in a long white dress and blue *tignon*, quietly laughing her head off. At first he thought she was just a poor old crazy woman. But then she spoke to him in an eerie, echoing voice.

"Don't you *know* me?" When Elmore said he didn't, she hauled off and hit him across the face, her eyes burning like hot coals.

An instant later she floated up off the floor, flew out the door, soared up over the light wires, then whizzed out of sight beyond the walls of the St. Louis Cemetery No. 1.

Elmore fainted. When he came to, the drugstore

owner was pouring whiskey down him. "You know who that was?" he asked Elmore. "You know who that *was?* Marie Laveau!"

Elmore shuddered. He knew who Marie Laveau was all right. The queen of the voodoos. She had been dead for more years than most people could remember. But her cantankerous spirit still raged about New Orleans, and *that* was what had whopped him across the face.

New Orleans is a city of ghosts, but none is so fascinating as that of Marie Laveau, the beautiful quadroon who reigned as voodoo queen for more than half a century. When was she born? When and how did she die? Or *did* she die? It is said that she was presiding over the famous slave dances in Congo Square as early as 1830; yet others have sworn they saw her, still handsome and vigorous, performing her terrible snake dance on St. John's Bayou as late as 1895.

She is supposed to have been kissed by Lafayette in 1825, and nearly a century later, to have been the mistress of a famous judge. Some say she perished in a hurricane, others that she dropped dead during a Mardi Gras ball. And still others believe that Marie Laveau never died at all, but changed herself to a big black crow that can still be seen flapping over St. Louis No. 1 Cemetery. You can tell it's no ordinary crow, they say, because of the way its head-feathers stick up in tufts. In life, Marie Laveau always wore a *tignon* — a kerchief tied in seven knots with the points sticking straight up.

It's easy to believe that Marie Laveau could turn herself into a crow if she chose, for from what we know of her she possessed extraordinary powers. In the 1800s the practice of voodoo was strictly forbidden in New Orleans, and yet Marie never got into trouble with the police. When they tried to break up her secret rites in Congo Square or on the banks of St. John's Bayou, Marie "hypnotized" them so that they either joined in the orgy or left her in peace. One witness claimed that the voodoo queen could make policemen get down on all fours and bark like dogs!

Even judges were not immune to her spells. Early in her career a young man of aristocratic family was accused of a crime, and his father appealed to Marie for help. A devout Catholic in spite of her witchcraft, she went to St. Louis Cathedral and knelt before the altar with three Guinea peppers under her tongue. Then, just before the trial, she slipped the three peppers under the judge's chair. Even though the evidence against the young man was strong, the judge acquitted him — and the grateful father rewarded Marie with a little house on St. Ann Street, which became the center of her voodoo rites. Here she sold *gris-gris* (little black magic pouches), cast spells, laid and lifted curses, told fortunes, mixed love potions, and became famous.

Almost everyone was afraid of Marie Laveau, and mothers would frighten unruly children into good behavior by threatening them with her name. It was rumored that her house was filled with black cats, spiders, trained roosters, bats. She had a snake named Zombi that she fed on watermelons — or human blood. Some people swore that she killed unwanted babies and roasted them on barbecue spits, and that she literally had skeletons in her closet. Bones from these skeletons, along with such unsavory items as dried frogs, cemetery dirt, and cat's eyes, she would sew into her *gris-gris* bags.

Frightened or not, customers flocked to Marie's door — poor black slaves and lovelorn ladies of high degree, politicians seeking office, even ministers who wanted help in filling their empty pews.

Marie's fame increased through her championship of prisoners condemned to death. She liked to cheat the gallows, and at least once fed a prisoner poisoned gumbo the night before he was due to hang. Another time a murderer whose cell she had often visited was saved from the hangman's noose when a messenger galloped up at the very last minute with a mysterious reprieve.

Her best-known gallows trick, though not exactly successful from the prisoners' standpoint, was certainly dramatic. Two Frenchmen she had vowed to save were standing on the platform with ropes already about their necks when the sunny skies darkened abruptly, lightning flashed and thunder crashed, rain flooded down, spectators screamed, and although the rattled executioner managed to release the trap door, both nooses slipped off the prisoners' necks and they landed on the ground bruised but alive. The panic-stricken crowd, not sure whether to credit this phenomenon to Marie or to God, bolted out of the square, trampling a number of fainting women and children. The unfortunate prisoners were later put to death, but that traumatic day marked the end of public executions in New Orleans.

Marie Laveau was probably most notorious for her part in the mysterious secret rites that took place each St. John's Eve on the banks of Lake Ponchartrain on St. John's Bayou. Here, at the Voodoo Festival, she gyrated wildly with her twenty-foot snake, sacrificed roosters, prayed over a black coffin. Her followers, black and white, were said to dance naked, to engage in dark rituals too horrible to describe. The whole place, people said, looked like a scene out of hell, with the bonfires, the torches, the leaping dancers, the smell of hot blood. At the height of the orgy, everyone plunged into the water — all except Marie Laveau, who walked *on* it.

It was at one of these Voodoo Festivals in the 1890s that Marie was supposedly drowned. There was a hurricane, and some said the voodoo queen was swept away with many of her followers. But not everyone believed the story. Others swore she was found days or weeks later — either clinging to a log, or sitting upright in the fork of a floating tree, or perched on a rooftop singing voodoo songs. "Marie Laveau, she's still alive!"

Actually, the "real" Marie Laveau probably died in 1881, and had possibly stopped her voodoo practices long before that date. Most historians now agree that there were *two* Marie Laveaus, the second being the original voodoo queen's daughter.

No one is sure exactly when Marie II began to take over from her mother, but the transition was so gradual that most people were not aware of the change. Although Marie I's death was reported in the New Orleans newspaper (rumors of earthquakes, thunderstorms, and other ghostly phenomena coinciding with that death), Marie II seems simply to have faded away. No one knows when she died or where she is buried, although there are two tombs, one in St. Louis Cemetery No. 1 and another in St. Louis No. 2, where believers still come to leave offerings of flowers, *gris-gris*, and coins — and to mark crosses on the stones with chips of red brick.

And, inevitably, there are spectral appearances. Is it Marie I or Marie II who materializes in the form of a large Newfoundland dog? A snake? A wraithlike form floating up and down St. Ann Street? A crazily laughing old lady in a drugstore? Then there is the strange crow with the tufted head-feathers, a robber crow that is said to fly in the windows of houses near the cemetery and make off with bits of gold jewelry. Those who have seen this apparition are probably seeing the ghost of Marie I, for it was she who wore the seven-knotted *tignon*, and long looped earrings.

On St. John's Eve, people who live along the bayou swear they have heard a mysterious singing in the wind, and those who dare peek through their windows may glimpse a shadowy shape that looks like a woman clinging to a floating log.

And this, they say, is the second Marie Laveau, floating off to a ghostly Voodoo Festival.

"Old Hickory"
and the Bell Witch

It wasn't a bear although it was about the *size* of a young bear. It wasn't a wolf. Or a wildcat.

John Bell scratched his head. The animal was unlike any he had ever seen. Certainly it was unlike anything he'd heard tell of in these parts — north-central Tennessee, Robertson County to be specific, just below the Kentucky state line.

There'd been no talk lately of a wild beast on the loose. And to tell the truth, this animal, strange as it was, did not look particularly wild *or* beastly. Yet there it sat, smack in the middle of his cornfield, showered in the late golden light of Indian summer. It made no sound, no movement, but sat calmly, *knowingly*, John Bell thought. There was an eerie human look about the face. An intelligence in the eyes, as though the animal had sized up John Bell and was enjoying his uneasiness.

Nothing to take chances with, Bell decided. He raised his gun, got the thing in his sights, was about to pull the trigger when, to his astonishment, the animal began dissolving — not stealing away, not moving — but *melting* into the air like a lump of snow in warm water.

John Bell stared for a moment at the place where it had sat. He moved closer, examined the ground. There were no tracks, no flattened weeds, no sign whatever that the soil had been disturbed. Bell checked the bushes at the edge of the field, poked them with a stick. No sign there either of an animal.

Mystifying. He decided he would say nothing about the incident to his family. No need to concern them. His eyes must have been playing tricks. It was a single incident. And it was over.

But it *wasn't*. Several days later, as he was crossing that same cornfield, John Bell saw perched on a split-rail fence a black bird of monstrous size. A wild turkey? A vulture? The creature was bigger than either. And it, like the animal he had encountered earlier, had an unnerving, *human* gaze.

Again John Bell raised his gun. This time there was no dissolving of matter into mist or thin air. The great bird casually unfolded its wings and flapped across the field, casting a shadow across skeletal corn stalks that chilled John Bell's blood. It was as though he had glimpsed, fleetingly, the shadow of death.

That was how it all began — more than a hundred and fifty years ago — the strange, four-year bedevilment that actually *did* send John Bell to his grave. A curse that was — is — expected to haunt one Bell in each generation. It was a time of torture Tennesseans still talk about. It was the time of the "Bell Witch."

Who . . . what . . . was the Bell Witch? Why did it single out John Bell, a kindly, hard-working Christian beloved by both family and community? Why did it disrupt his household for four agonizing years? Terrorize every one of his eight children? Focus its hostilities upon the lovely, teenage Elizabeth (Betsy), harass her to the point that she almost lost her mind and *did* lose the man she loved? Why did it afflict all who visited the Bell farm, even President-to-be Andrew Jackson, who journeyed up from the Hermitage near Nashville? And why, moreover, did it spare John Bell's wife, Lucy? Why was she, alone, in the witch's good graces?

No one could — *can* — explain although many have tried to account for the four years of bedlam that began with the appearances of the "human" animal and monster bird in John Bell's cornfield.

Shortly afterward, eerie scratchings were heard at the doors and windows of the Bell house as though some clawed creature wanted in. Then, quite suddenly, the creature *was* in, tearing away at the bedposts, the floors, sometimes with such frenzy that the house rocked with earthquake fury. Bedcovers would be snatched from the Bell children at night, their hair would be pulled, noses pinched and faces slapped. "The blows were distinctly heard," the youngest son, Williams Bell, noted in the diary he wrote some years later. "Like the open palm of a heavy hand."

The first time he was attacked, young Williams Bell said it felt as if the whole top of his head were being ripped off. His brother Joel in the bed next to him screamed out in pain, and then Betsy in her room down the hall. "Something was continually pulling at her hair after she retired to bed," Williams Bell wrote.

At first the Bells kept their troubles secret. The attacks would pass, John Bell believed. But they did not pass. On the contrary. They intensified so alarmingly that he, a man not easily shaken, was driven to seek help. The man he approached was their nearest neighbor and close friend, a lay preacher named James Johnson. Johnson came at once to the Bell farm, heard for himself the scrabblings of claws, the smacking of lips, the curious whistling of air being sucked through snaggled teeth. He stood in the living room, arms outstretched, and addressed the noises, as though they were human: "Stop, I beseech you, in the name of the Lord."

The noises did cease. For several weeks. But they began again, more violent than ever. Johnson, summoned back to the Bell house, again addressed the noises. Whenever he spoke, the noises would stop, as though listening. But as soon as he had finished speaking, they would resume. In answer? It seemed so. Whoever — whatever — was causing the noises, Johnson concluded, was human. Or at least of human intelligence.

His theory proved to be right. The noises soon became intelligible. The ghost or witch spoke words the Bells could understand, torrents aimed, in particular, at John Bell and young Betsy.

"This vile, heinous, unknown devil," wrote Williams Bell in his diary, "this torturer of human flesh, that preyed upon the fears of people like a ravenous vulture, spared her not but rather chose her as a shining mark for an exhibition of its wicked stratagem and devilish tortures." So plagued was Betsy that she was packed off to neighbors in hopes that she would be unmolested there. But such was not the case. The witch simply followed Betsy, throwing one neighbor's, then another's house into chaos. Strangely, the Bell house remained under attack even in Betsy's absence. The witch could hold forth in two places at once.

Word about the Bell Witch spread fast. The curious crowded into the Bell farm, remaining well into the night to hear — and, hopefully, to see — the witch. They would command it to rap on the wall, to smack its lips, to whistle, to speak. And the witch invariably would accommodate them. Before long, there were question-and-answer sessions: Who was the witch? Where did it come from? Why did it come? Why was it invisible? Was it alive? Was it dead?

One night the witch answered: "I am a Spirit from everywhere. From Heaven, Hell, the Earth. I'm in the air, in houses, *any* place at *any* time. I've been created millions of years."

On another occasion it confessed, solemnly, that it was the spirit of one who had been wronged, which led some to believe that the witch might be the spirit of old Kate Batts from whom John Bell had bought his property. Old Kate maintained that John Bell had cheated her in the deal, that he, a wealthy man, had taken advantage of her, a poor, hard-working woman, by paying her a good deal less than her property was worth.

Not long afterward the disembodied voice flatly announced, "I am nothing more or less than old Kate Batts' witch, and I'm determined to haunt and torment 'Old Jack' (as she called John Bell) as long as he lives."

But Kate Batts was very much alive at the time of the shenanigans. A *spirit* she was not. But a witch? Some say she was. She was a local character, certainly, disliked by the majority. And she did, indeed, have it in for John Bell.

By now she — the witch — had become vociferous. And something of a religious fanatic. She called Preacher Johnson "Old Sugar Mouth" (because of the sweetness of his sermons) and made a point of attending every revival, screaming "Amens" and "Hallelujahs" above the congregation. "Lord Jesus," she cried once, "how sweet Old Sugar Mouth prays. How I *do* love to hear him."

She then discovered that whiskey was even more to her taste than Old Sugar Mouth and her voice became harsher, wilder than ever. One moonshiner, then another claimed that she raided his stillhouse. Certainly she flounced about Robertson County roaring drunk, returning always to the Bell farm to bedevil "Old Jack" and Betsy.

It was at about this time that Betsy and young Josiah Gardener discovered one another. He was a Robertson County boy of good family, diligent, hard working and devoted to Betsy. It seemed a good match. Both families were delighted. But not Old Kate, as everyone now called the witch.

"Please, Betsy Bell, don't have Josiah Gardener," Old Kate pleaded. She then set about bedeviling the pair, uttering obscenities wherever they went, especially when others were present. She promised Betsy "no rest" if she married Josiah.

By now tales of the Bell Witch's antics had spread clear across central Tennessee, from the Kentucky border past Nashville to Alabama. General Andrew Jackson, who then lived at the Hermitage, a plantation some few miles east of Nashville, heard the stories and determined to drive up to the Bell farm to have a look for himself. He, who had defeated the

Creek Indians in 1814 at the Battle of Horseshoe
Bend, who had become a national hero by winning
the Battle of New Orleans in 1815, who had faced
the Seminole in 1818, would now confront the "terror" at the Bell farm and with the help of a "witch-
layer" he had located, "lay" it to rest forever.

Jackson filled his wagon with friends and set out in
high spirits for the Bell farm in Robertson County, a
journey in those days of perhaps forty or fifty miles.
Just as he crossed the Bell property line, his wagon
bumped to a halt. The mules groaned and strained,
Jackson swore, but the wagon held fast as though
mired in mud. But there was no mud. There was
nothing, in fact, to impede the way.

Suddenly a voice wafted in on the air, "All right,
General, the wagon can move on."

And, sure enough, as if a brake had magically been
released, the wagon catapulted forward and rumbled
across the fields toward the Bell house.

"By thunder," Jackson roared. "It's the witch."

It was indeed. It was also quite a show the witch
staged that night for General Jackson, hurling dishes
across the living room, flinging furniture about as
though it were mere chips of wood, ripping bedcovers from the beds of guests, singing . . . swearing
. . . taunting.

"All right, General," she challenged Jackson
shortly after dinner. "Here I am, ready for business."

She turned then to the witch-layer Jackson had brought. "All right, Smarty. Shoot." (The belief then was that any phantom, witch, devil or ghost, if struck in the heart by a silver bullet, would be silenced forever.)

The witch-layer raised his pistol and squeezed the trigger. It jammed.

"*Again*," shrilled Old Kate. "Fire again." Again the gun jammed.

"It's my turn *now*," she screamed. "Look out, you old hypocrite." A loud report coursed through the house, the sound of a gun fired at close range. The witch-layer fell to the floor, writhing in pain.

"My nose, my nose. It's got me by the nose." He then fled from the house, never to be seen again.

It was a weary Jackson who bade the Bells good-bye the following morning.

"I'd rather fight the British again," he said, "than have any more dealings with that torment."

Jackson rid himself of the torment simply by leaving the Bell farm. The Bells, however, were stuck with it.

Not long after Jackson's departure, John Bell began having "spells." Convulsions, they would probably be called today. He would twitch, roll his eyes, and his tongue would swell inside his mouth, very nearly choking him to death. The spells continued, month after month, increasing with each seizure in severity and duration.

Finally, John Bell admitted that the end was near. "My son," he announced one day to Williams, his youngest, "this thing is killing me." He retreated to his bed.

A few days later, young Williams found his father in a coma. He found, too, that medicine the family doctor had prescribed had been replaced by a vial of evil, fuming liquid. He called the doctor, who, as a test, dipped a straw into the mysterious vial, then touched it to the tongue of a cat. The cat spun round as if possessed, flopped on its side, twitched violently, then died.

"Old Jack'll never get up," the witch screamed. "I gave him a big dose out of that same vial last night. *That* fixed him!"

It did, indeed. John Bell died the next morning. It was December 21, 1820. The witch had made good her promise, to haunt John Bell to his grave. Literally, for as John Bell's body was being lowered into the ground, the witch sang out:

"Row me up some brandy, oh."

John Bell's death, together with Betsy Bell's broken engagement, broke the witch's spell. One evening, not long afterward, as the Bells sat by the fire, a boulder rolled down the chimney and out into the living room: "Good-bye," it said. "I am going and will be gone for seven years." The harassment stopped as abruptly as it had begun. For the first time in four years, the Bell family was at peace.

Seven years later there was a clawing at the doors and windows. *Outside.* The Bells held their breaths, said nothing of the disturbances, and within two weeks, they subsided.

During this time the witch *spoke* at the home of John Bell, Jr., vowing to return exactly one hundred and seven years later.

The people of Robertson County continued to report strange noises, unexplained lights, bursts of flame in the vicinity of the Bell farm. The place was haunted, they swore, even after the house had been demolished.

The Bell family, however, insisted that they saw, heard, felt nothing. The one hundred and seven years passed without incident. And almost forty years more.

Still, the witch *has* vowed to return. To visit descendants of "Old Jack" Bell.

Who can say? One day, perhaps, the witch *will* return. Meanwhile, the descendants can only wonder. And wait.

The Wizard's Revenge

On a blustery night nearly two hundred years ago, a Mr. and Mrs. Livingstone of Middleway, West Virginia, were roused by a sharp rap at their door — not an unusual occurrence for the couple, living as they did along the old Baltimore-Kentucky trail.

But there was desperation in this particular knock.

"Don't answer," Mrs. Livingstone warned her husband. It was a wretched night, with sleet peppering the windows and wind whooshing down the chimney, and Mrs. Livingstone had no intention of abandoning the snug warmth of her featherbed. Whoever it was would soon move on if his knock went unanswered.

But the knock persisted and Livingstone gave in to it, despite his wife's objections.

As he opened the door a crack, a bony hand scrabbled in. And then, as if driven by a tornado, a man in a dark cloak spun into the room.

"Sir," he began when he had steadied himself, "my

wagon has thrown a wheel. I pray you can give me lodging for the night."

"Gladly," Livingstone replied and welcomed the stranger in, though Mrs. Livingstone, now out of bed too, scowled from the bedroom doorway. Grumbling, she made room for the stranger. What was it about her husband, she wondered, that made him so quick to befriend strangers? There were highwaymen about, killers, lunatics, Indians. Did he not realize she could be murdered in her bed?

With the stranger settled, the Livingstones retired once more. But before they could sink into sleep, a cry tore through the night.

"The wind," Mrs. Livingstone said, putting out a hand to restrain her husband. But the cry came again. Piercingly human. Livingstone bolted from bed and found the stranger rigid with pain.

"S-summon a priest," he managed. "I am dying."

"Nonsense!" snorted Mrs. Linvingstone, standing now by her husband. "Besides, there are no priests hereabouts."

"But the McSherries," her husband protested. "Perhaps they know of one. I'll go ask."

"You'll do no such thing. You are not going out in this night. And if you do, I will not let you — and certainly no Romish priest — set foot in my house."

"But the stranger . . ."

"Merely cramped from the cold. I'll wager he'll be up and out before us."

So Livingstone returned to bed once again and as his wife had predicted, the cries soon subsided. Next morning, Livingstone looked in on the stranger.

He was dead.

There was a simple graveside ceremony. Livingstone did not even know the stranger's name. He had not asked, and there were no papers of identification. A few neighbors, told only that the stranger had died peacefully in his sleep, helped lay him to rest.

But the stranger's soul would not rest.

No sooner had the Livingstones come home from the burial than the logs in their fireplace began to writhe and cry out in pain. One by one, they sailed out of the hearth and round the room, comets trailing tails of fire. The Livingstones scrambled after them, terrified that their house would go up in smoke, but as fast as they replaced a log on the fire it would hurl itself back into the room. There was no sleep that night.

The following morning, a stagedriver confronted Livingstone in front of his house.

"How dare you rope off the road barring my way?"

"But there *is* no rope," and in truth, Livingstone could see none.

The driver slashed at the rope with his knife, watched astonished as it passed through the rope without severing it. He then stepped easily through the rope himself. Assuming this to be the work of the devil, he swung aboard the stage, took a whip to the horses and lurched down the trail at a gallop.

For weeks thereafter every wagon to approach the Livingstones was stopped by the rope and every wagoneer cursed Livingstone. After the first few encounters, Livingstone decided it would be easier to pretend to cut the rope than to explain that it was a *phantom* rope strung up by a ghost. The plan, of course, was futile because Livingstone himself never saw the rope and so, again and again, he was forced to relate the story of the stranger who had died "peacefully" in his sleep that grim and icy night.

At the same time, the Livingstones were being plagued by noises in the house. Moans, bone-chilling cries and an incessant *clip-clip, snip-snip, clip-clip*, as though giant scissors were cutting cloth. Suddenly holes appeared in the Livingstones' linens and clothes, all of them neat crescent moons.

Tales of the mysterious snipping passed from neighbor to neighbor, then sped through the valleys of West Virginia until the curious were coming from as far afield as Virginia and Maryland to hear the "wizard," as the ghost was now known, busy with his shears. Moreover, many of them departed victims, although few realized it until later when they reached for their pocket handkerchiefs and found them riddled with crescent moons.

On a dare, a young braggart rode twenty miles to

the Livingstone house from Winchester, Virginia, to prove he was man enough to spook the ghost. He wasn't, as the knot of spectators quickly learned. The boy swaggered into the house, began taunting the ghost, but cowered and fled the instant the wizard reached down unseen and snipped out the seat of his pants.

The Livingstones were not amused. Mrs. Livingstone, steelier by nature than her husband, was horrorstruck the day she watched the wizard decapitate her ducks, one after the other, on the lawn in front of her guests.

The ghost must be exorcised. But how? By whom?

That night a man in black visited Livingstone in a dream. He stood in a silver light above the stranger's grave, his robes blown out behind him like wings. A voice addressed Livingstone, not the voice of the man in black but a disembodied voice gusting in on the wind. The man in black was a priest, the voice said, come to put an end to the wizard and his tricks.

Livingstone rose the next day resolved to locate a priest. From his neighbors the McSherries he learned that a Father Cahill would be coming in a day or two to say mass at Shepherdstown, ten miles distant.

Livingstone rode to Shepherdstown and upon seeing Father Cahill, gasped and collapsed. The face of the priest was the face of the man in black.

Regaining consciousness, Livingstone sobbed out the story, confessing to Father Cahill his guilt and his wife's, castigating them both for their inhumanity and negligence. Father Cahill listened, then agreed to follow Livingstone home and do what he could about quieting the vengeful spirit.

At Livingstone's door he knelt and whispered a prayer over a small cross clutched in his hands. Then he sprinkled the threshold with holy water.

"Now lead me to the grave," he said.

The two men climbed the hill behind Livingstone's house to the clearing. Father Cahill stood as he had in the dream and consecrated the grave. Suddenly a wind ripped through the trees sending down torrents of leaves. And the waters of the lake beyond rose in a dark wave, broke, then lay still.

His deed done, Father Cahill departed and for the first time in months peace settled upon the countryside. The Livingstones were so grateful they deeded thirty-four acres of their property, including that where the stranger lay buried, to Father Cahill and all priests who would succeed him.

The deed is filed today among the records of the Charles Town, West Virginia, County Courthouse and though fragile and faded, it is still legible. The thirty-four-acre tract is known yet as Priest Field and old-timers born and bred where it all happened call the town of Middleway "Wizard Clip," because, they insist, when the night grows dark and blustering, the wizard can still be heard clipping away.

It may be so.

The Strange, Sad Spirit
of the Scioto

He came out of the wilderness near Delaware, Ohio, a hundred and fifty years ago — unannounced, unknown, uncommunicative. A few years later he vanished, leaving behind a moldering mansion . . . an empty tomb crawling with snakes, spiders and salamanders . . . a community beset by rumors of buried treasure and murder.

He also left the community a ghost. Not his own, but that of a young Spanish girl who had appeared mysteriously in Delaware County exactly two years after the man, then disappeared with even greater mystery.

She was murdered, it's said. Neighbors had heard shrieks of terror and pain, sobs and wails. Then they had heard nothing. And they had *seen* nothing of the Spanish girl until that summery afternoon, months later, when her ghostly figure glided along the willow-laced banks of the Scioto River.

But we are getting ahead of our story.

It all began in 1825 when a man named John Rob-

inson left a party of trappers at Delaware, Ohio, on
the path of portage between the Ohio River and the
town of Sandusky on Lake Erie. Robinson wasn't a
trapper. Or even a friend of the trappers with whom
he traveled, for when he left them at Delaware they
parted without good-byes or good wishes.

Delaware Village at the time was scarcely even
that — a few log huts lined up beside a rutted road, a
general store, a blacksmith shop and stable, a tavern.
Robinson put in at the tavern, lugging with him two
enormous, leaden sacks. He was silent, secretive, vol-
unteering no information and seeking none other
than where in the vicinity he might rent a sturdy
saddle horse.

The next day, on a horse hired at the smithy's,
Robinson set off for the bottomlands and bluffs of
south Delaware County. It was — is yet wherever
industry has not encroached — lush country. Cliffy,
thickly forested, with the broad Scioto meandering
through. Beyond the high bluffs, farmlands roll
south in shades of green toward the city of Colum-
bus beyond the horizon.

A peaceful retreat is what Robinson sought. And
he found it in south Delaware County, a piece of
bottomland by the Scioto, and above it a wooded,
clifftop aerie.

That night, back in Delaware Village, Robinson
negotiated to buy the property, a parcel of consider-
able acreage. Once the deal was sealed, the deed

signed, Robinson began designing a house grander than any Delaware County had ever seen. It was an immense country estate, sprawling the entire length of the bluff, a house bigger by far than any yet built in Ohio.

Presently masons, carpenters and artisans began arriving from New York and other eastern cities, and before long the skeleton of a mansion rose in the forest. Delaware County watched with fascination as giant stones were blasted out of a hillside, then meticulously cut and shaped for the facade. They watched, too, as Robinson himself carved intricate cornices, mantels and wainscotting out of felled oaks. A master craftsman he, better than any they'd seen.

For months the construction continued. And for months the people of Delaware County watched . . . and wondered . . . and waited. For the housewarming. For the rounds of socializing that would inevitably follow the opening of such a great house.

But none was forthcoming. When the final brushstroke was made, the last nail driven, Robinson dismissed the workmen, withdrew inside his fine new home and bolted the door. He received no one except wagoners from New York hauling in loads of furniture he had imported from England and Europe.

Neighbors, town officials, local workmen who had lent a hand, were understandably puzzled. And miffed. Robinson had used them, then rejected them. Those few well-meaning villagers who came to call, to welcome Robinson formally to the community, were brusquely turned away.

Gossip flew. About Robinson, his mansion, his unending source of money. Those who had actually been inside the great house, for the most part workmen who had helped build it, spun wild tales of gilded furniture, diamond-bright chandeliers, damasks and brocades. It was an opulence both unseen and out of place in the Ohio wilderness of the early nineteenth century. The workmen also marveled at the pictures they had seen Robinson painting. He was a fine artist, they said, who spent his days filling canvas after canvas with the likenesses of beautiful women.

Soon the walls of the great house were covered with Robinson's paintings. One, in particular, caught the eye of a craftsman who had been summoned to make a repair. It was a canvas so massive it occupied one entire wall of the studio-library. It was a group portrait, its setting the deck of a pirate ship. To port stood the seamen, to starboard the officers. And in the middle of the deck — swaggering in gold-braided uniform — stood the pirate captain.

It was Robinson. The spitting image, the workman insisted.

Suddenly the people of Delaware County began to shun Robinson as he had shunned them. No one trespassed upon his property. No one dared enter his drive. The superstitious were so terrified they traveled miles out of their way rather than skirt Robinson's boundary line.

A pirate captain! And in their very midst. But what of Robinson's love of art, music and books (strange pursuits for a swashbuckler)? That riddle seemed solved by other paintings of Robinson's, which, more often than not, were set on the grounds of some vast country estate, in a great hall or ballroom. Robinson, the local folk suspected, was the black sheep of a noble English family. A prodigal son. That would account for his extravagant tastes. As for the weighty bags he had first lugged into Delaware Village, there was no doubt now as to what they had contained. Gold! And the iron-bound chests brought in with the furniture? More gold. And no doubt silver and jewels as well.

Then, quite unexpectedly treasure of another sort appeared at the estate — a lovely young girl. Like Robinson's own arrival, hers was unseen, unannounced, unexplained. She might very well have dropped out of the sky. There was an exotic, foreign look about her, said those who had glimpsed her in the forest: eyes and hair black as ebony, pale complexion ever so faintly tinged with olive. She might be a Spanish princess captured by Robinson in his days of buccaneering. Or a countess. Or the daughter of a wealthy West Indian planter.

In the beginning, as long as summer spread its warmth and light throughout the forest, the girl seemed happy. She could be seen there, wandering childlike, whenever Robinson did not demand her services as a model. Her favorite haunts were the banks of the Scioto and a rocky perch high above that Robinson had carved into the face of the bluff.

When autumn overtook summer, however, and then winter autumn, she withdrew inside the mansion, a forlorn tropical flower withering in an alien land. It was then that her direful shrieks pierced the forest, bone-numbing cries heard clear across the southern end of Delaware County. Word spread that Robinson was a cruel master, that he tormented and beat the poor girl whenever she displeased him.

Then, as abruptly as they had begun, the cries subsided. Winter settled in, cloaking the forests in silence and snow. Delaware County folk, busy with their own chores, left the recluse Robinson to his own. They talked, of course, of Robinson around their fires at night, of the strange, sad little *señorita*, of the melancholy mansion and of the eerie goings-on there.

Spring came at last, awakening the forest. But not the mansion. It remained ominously silent. A mansion of the dead. Neighbors began to wonder. And to speculate. Before long, before the forest was in full leaf, all of Delaware County buzzed with excitement.

Weeks, months had passed without sight or sound of Robinson or the Spanish girl. Vines had begun creeping up the gray stone face of the mansion, sending tendrils over the windowpanes. Weeds sprang into the drive — wilderness reclaiming its territory.

For all the talk, however, no one dared go up to the great house. But, eventually, curiosity overpowered fear and a group of lusty plowmen joined forces to investigate. They approached the mansion one sunny summer midday, singing and joking as if to wake the dead.

The dead did not rouse. The mansion slumbered on, silent, sinister. When their knocks went unanswered, they improvised a battering ram out of a fallen tree, and beat the door down.

No sign of life whatever. The mansion stood empty, untouched, elegant — *except* for the library. With chairs, tables and easels overturned, with canvasses mutilated, it looked like a battlefield. Bloody fingerprints reached up one wall toward a single, unscathed painting — a portrait of the Spanish girl.

The men stared at it incredulously, for under their very gaze its colors seemed to shift and intensify. Light flickered in the black eyes, the lips parted . . . as if to speak . . .

Then, ever so softly, came the sound of sobbing. The men bolted and ran top speed all the way to Delaware Village, shouting that the mansion was haunted. That night — and every night thereafter — agonizing moans welled up out of the midnight stillness of the forest.

For weeks no one would venture near the place. But then people began talking again of buried treasure, and greed quickly got the better of ghostly fears.

The hunt was on. Whole caravans lumbered onto the estate grounds, men bearing picks, sledgehammers, shovels, saws and axes. Day after day (for no one was brave enough to tarry after the sun had gone down), they hacked away at the very foundations of the mansion. Robinson's coffin was discovered, a gruesomely chased oaken box that Robinson himself had carved. It stood empty, as did the gray stone tomb he had built as his final resting place on a knoll behind the house.

For months the search continued, growing more and more frenzied, until the great house began to sag, to crack and to crumble. The roof collapsed, the sweeping stair fell, ceilings and walls stood bare. Time soon finished what the treasure-seekers had begun. The once proud house was reduced to rubble, but it withheld still the whereabouts of Robinson's treasure. Not a single golden sovereign was ever found.

In the end, nothing remained of the great house Robinson had raised in the forest. Of the lavish furnishings he had imported from Europe. Of the canvasses he had painted. Of Robinson himself, who had slipped back into the wilderness of central Ohio as stealthily as he had emerged from it.

Only the Spanish lady lingered — *in spirit.*
Dressed in brocades and lace, she would appear in
the golden light of late afternoon to wander along
the Scioto, to climb to her stone perch, to fly
through the forest to the mansion site. Sitting atop
the rubble she would begin sobbing and then, as if
mired in quicksand, would sink slowly, dissolving, it
seemed, into shades of dusk.

Day after day it was thus. For a hundred years or
more.

Some old-timers swear that she comes yet, adding
that if you want to glimpse her you must come of a
summer afternoon about five o'clock . . . come to
the banks of the Scioto just north of the Franklin-
Delaware County line . . . come to the river's-edge
fringe of willows . . . come prepared to wait . . .

And then . . . maybe, just maybe . . . you will
see her, ever so shadowy, ever so silent.

The "Spirited" Librarian

He hadn't meant to take the book from the library. He certainly hadn't meant to keep it overnight. But the poems, strange and exotic verses penned in India late in the eighteenth century, were so fascinating he simply slipped the slim volume off the shelf and into his pocket so that he could study them more carefully. He'd intended returning the book to the shelf that day, but as so often happens, he became absorbed, time whizzed by, and before he knew it, it was too late — the library had closed.

So there he was in his dormitory room, holding a rare and valuable work, a first edition, and worse still, one from the Whitcomb Library. This priceless collection of books had been bequeathed to DePauw University by Indiana Governor James Whitcomb, who had spent a lifetime amassing it. Whitcomb, in fact, so cherished his books he stipulated in his will that they were "to be used as reference work only," that "none of them should under any conditions be removed from the library building."

Occasionally one of the books would find its way out of the library, usually when a new assistant would blithely sign it out, unaware of the special restrictions put upon the Whitcomb books.

But the young student knew the rules, which accounted for his apprehension now. And had he known the background of *The Poems of Oison*, the book he had "borrowed," he might have been a good bit more apprehensive. The poems — both mystical and mysterious — had been written in India, published in Philadelphia in 1789, passed from hand to hand, then brought in 1813 into the Indiana Territory by oxcart and flatboat as a gift for young James Whitcomb who would one day serve Indiana as Governor (and for whom the "Hoosier Poet," James Whitcomb Riley, would be named. Riley's father had served in the Indiana General Assembly during Whitcomb's term of office.)

It was now the early 1900s, so the book the student held in his hands was more than a hundred years old, a dusty, yellowing, far from imposing volume. Yet the poems had lost none of their magic, and the young man sat up well past midnight, spellbound by the Indian images and messages.

When at last he did retire, he tucked the book carefully under his pillow. Thoughts raced through his head in no particular pattern, and then it seemed he had no thoughts at all as down, down he sank, deep down into sleep.

Abruptly, he was yanked up out of sleep by . . . what was it? A knocking at the door? Lines from Edgar Allan Poe's poem "The Raven" flew through his head . . ." suddenly there came a tapping, as of some one gently rapping, rapping at his chamber door . . ."

At the foot of his bed hovered a spectral figure in funeral robes, a man almost as high as the ceiling, a man with bony arm outstretched pointing straight at his pillow.

"Oison! Oison!" the specter rasped. "Who stole Oison?" Then with menacing arm and clenched fist, the ghost struck out at the young student, cringing in bed.

Over and over again he intoned the words . . . eerily . . . chanting . . . "Oison! Oison! Who stole Oison? . . . O-i-s-o-n . . . O-i-s-o-n . . . w-h-o s-t-o-l-e O-i-s-o-n . . ." The words drifted away in the night as the specter itself seemed to dissolve.

Paralyzed with fright, the student shrank back against the headboard. He had actually felt the clammy, dead hand of Governor Whitcomb brush across his face. Unable to move or speak, he crouched for hours at the head of his bed, terrified that the specter might return. Finally, at day's first light, he reached under his pillow and withdrew the "borrowed" book.

He was at the library long before it opened. The instant the door was unlocked, he raced to the desk, words tumbling out at a bewildered librarian: "Here it is! Here is Oison!" With that, he broke down and confessed how he had slipped the book from the shelf and how the ghost of Governor Whitcomb had hovered over his bed most of the night.

A day or two later when the story was being told at one of the women's dormitories, a young girl leapt up.

"When," she gasped, "does the library close?"

When told at 5 P.M., she whirled out of the room, shouting, "I still have fifteen minutes!"

She, too, had "borrowed" one of the Whitcomb books.

In the old days — that is before 1956, when De-Pauw opened its spanking new library — librarians didn't worry very much about the Whitcomb collection. If one of the books was missing, they knew the "spirited" librarian would see that it was soon returned to its rightful place.

There haven't been stories recently of books missing from the Whitcomb collection. Or of the Governor's ghostly midnight walks. Still, that isn't to say the old man *won't* walk again — should someone decide to "borrow" a book.

Ghost Ship of the Great Lakes

They slip in and out of the fog, steal across the horizon, drift out of dawn into dusk, the Flying Dutchmen of the Great Lakes.

There are dozens of them, ships that vanished without a trace. All hands lost. These are the schooners and steamers forever doomed, destined never to reach safe harbor. They ride out the Lakes' November storms, weather the winter "lock-up" when ice jams shipping lanes and closes ports. These are the ghost ships, beating always against the wind — mirages in the mist, phantoms of the night, gray shadows against sea and sky.

These are the specters playing tricks with the eyes of Lake pilots, the marine disasters hung up in their memories: The *L. R. Doty*, young and seaworthy, out of Chicago bound for Midland, Ontario, vanished 1898 . . . the *W. H. Gilcher*, coal-laden steamer, disappeared 1892 near the Straits of Mackinac . . . the *Nashua*, 1901, down in Lake Huron without a trace . . . the *Celtic*, 1902, upbound to the

Soo, sailed off the map of the Lakes and into legend . . .

Every Lakeman knows these legends. He knows, too, the legend of La Salle's *Griffin*, the Great Lakes' first Flying Dutchman, has heard time and again how she "sailed through a crack in the ice" of Lake Michigan almost three hundred years ago.

The *Griffin* was a stout ship, a proud ship, built by the French explorer Robert Cavelier de La Salle. But she never completed her maiden voyage. Here is how it happened.

La Salle immigrated to Montreal from France in 1666. He was just twenty-three years old. From his king, Louis XIV, he had obtained grants of land and trading privileges in the "West" and from Count Frontenac, the French Governor of Quebec, the funds to back his explorations. La Salle quickly learned the language of the Indians, then with an Indian guide followed portages across the rolling lands of what is now Ohio and descended the Ohio River as far as Louisville, Kentucky.

La Salle was in the fur trade, a lucrative business, and to protect his interests against the intrusions of British traders and gain a toehold in the West, he began building a blockhouse just above Niagara Falls. A year later, in 1679, having obtained the right to "seek a water passage to the Gulf of Mexico," La Salle set about building at Niagara a magnificent sailing ship to carry him across the New

World's great inland waterway and to carry back the furs he bartered from Indian trappers.

The ship was not easily built. The Seneca Indians saw evil in the building of such a monster ship just as the Huron, some seventy years earlier, had associated doom with Champlain's forays up the St. Lawrence River. The Seneca refused to sell corn to the Frenchmen; they feigned attack. But despite their harassment, work progressed and a great ship was launched in Lake Erie. She was sixty feet long, of fifty to sixty tons burden, two-masted and many-sailed. Perched above her high, carved stern was a wooden eagle, wings spread for flight.

La Salle named his ship the *Griffin* after that fierce mythical beast, the winged lion with an eagle's head that would tear to shreds any horse or human being that barred its way. A prancing carved griffin was mounted on the ship's prow and all was ready for the maiden voyage across Lakes Erie, Huron and Michigan.

On August 7, 1679, the *Griffin* set sail. She was the Great Lakes' first commercial vessel, a leviathan in those days of birch and elm bark canoes. La Salle stood on the quarterdeck, proud and confident. His ship carried five cannon, a crew of thirty-two and a cargo of trinkets with which he would barter furs from the Indians.

In three calm days, the *Griffin* glided across Lake Erie, then nosed north into the Detroit River, skimmed across Lake St. Clair into the St. Clair River, then entered the broad waters of Lake Huron, second largest of the New World's mighty, freshwater "inland seas."

Abruptly, as so often happens on the Great Lakes, the weather shifted. A squall thundered out of Georgian Bay, gripped the *Griffin*, and hurled her against mountains of water. The Frenchmen, ocean seamen all, were unprepared for and terrified of the Lake's crashing walls of water. (It is true even today that ocean-going sailors become seasick on the Lakes; their freshwater waves, being less dense than the salt, pitch more sharply. Moreover, the Lakes are shallower than the oceans, smaller, with less room for stormy seas to roll and subside.)

The *Griffin* pitched dangerously as waves smashed across her high stern. The crew panicked, abandoned hopes of ever reaching land, dropped to its knees in prayer, and put its fate in the hands of the Almighty. All, that is, except La Salle and his doughty pilot, a veteran seaman who hissed epithets at La Salle, cursed him for "bringing him thither," causing him to perish in an *inland lake* thereby losing a glory hard won at sea.

Suddenly the winds and waves subsided as unpredictably as they had blustered out of Georgian Bay. The *Griffin*, undamaged despite ruthless battering by tumultuous seas, made her way serenely toward St. Ignace on the north shore of the Straits of Mackinac, a small outpost founded eight years earlier by Père Marquette.

From St. Ignace the *Griffin* cleared the Straits and headed south into Lake Michigan for Green Bay, where La Salle intended to take on a load of furs. The *Griffin* made Green Bay without incident, and there La Salle bartered from the Winnebago enough furs to make his fortune. They were laded into the *Griffin* along with provisions for the return voyage to Fort Niagara.

La Salle did not sail from Green Bay with the *Griffin* but set out instead for the St. Joseph River on the first lap of a voyage that would, he hoped, bring him to the Mississippi. That great river he would follow south to the sea — the Gulf of Mexico. (Six years earlier, Père Marquette, Louis Jolliet and a party of five had descended the Mississippi to the mouth of the Arkansas River.)

Though La Salle would make it to the mouth of the Mississippi, he did not do so this particular voyage. He turned back, in fact, short of the Mississippi River, at Starved Rock on the Illinois about sixty miles west of Chicago. He returned to Canada, covering one thousand miles by canoe and carry in sixty-five days.

Tragic news awaited him. The *Griffin* and her precious cargo of furs had never been heard of again.

She had set sail from Green Bay on September 18, 1679, bound for Niagara. The winds were light, out of the West, an auspicious beginning it would seem. But that was the last anyone saw of her.

The *Griffin* failed to reach the Straits of Mackinac (or, at least, failed to report). She never arrived (or rather, was never seen) at St. Ignace. Had she reached Lake Huron? Had another tempest there driven her to the bottom to the accompaniment of the Ottawa drum, that mysterious, legendary booming that is heard yet, tolling the number of lives lost on the Lakes? Had she reached Lake Erie? Or had she, simply, been swallowed up by Lake Michigan? "Sailed through a crack in the ice," as the story goes, never to be seen again — except as a ghost ship, looming out of the fog?

"Spook Light" of Devil's Promenade

In the southwest corner of Missouri, very near Joplin, within a whoop and a holler of both Kansas and Oklahoma, a rough unpaved road rollercoasters through a desolate stretch where jack oaks, scrubby and gnarled, reach skyward.

They might be witches, haggard, misshapen, performing a dance of death, especially if you see them on a black night with a river of mist swirling over the land.

"Devil's Promenade," locals call this road. And for good reason.

Every night, in fair weather and foul, an eerie ball of fire bounces down the road from west to east. It moves, always, in an easterly direction. Never the reverse.

Any stranger tarrying in these parts will soon be asked, "Have you seen the Spook Light?" Or, "Would you like to see the Hornet Ghost Light, the Devil's Jack-o'-Lantern?"

The fireball looks sometimes like a phosphorescent

jack-o'-lantern. At others, an incandescent egg. No
two persons ever see the ghostly light quite the same
way. To some it is a giant pumpkin, rollicking along
the corrugated road, bouncing occasionally as high as
the scraggly jack oak branches. To others, it is a
small piercing sun. Or a cluster of shooting stars
whizzing down the road. Sometimes the light glows
green. Sometimes it is red or yellow or blue. But
mostly it is a ghostly, silver light.

What is it? *Who* is it? No one can say although
there are legends by the dozen to account for what
science has been unable to explain — even in this day
of moon walks and space labs.

The Devil's Promenade, old-timers will tell you,
was once the stomping ground of the Quapaw Indians and here, many, many moons ago, a young brave
and Indian maiden fell in love. They planned to
marry, but the girl's father, a greedy chief, demanded
more in the way of a dowry than the young brave
could afford. So, rather than be parted, the lovers
stole away. The chief, however, was onto their plan
and dispatched a party of warriors. They overtook
the elopers at the crest of a bluff above the Spring
River, then watched in horror as the pair twisted free
and leaped to their death. It was shortly afterward,
in 1866, that the mysterious light was first seen along
Devil's Promenade. The young lovers back from the
dead, the Indians said.

Others seeing the ghost light thought it to be the

spirit of a lonely miner who had vanished one night without a trace while trying to locate his lucky strike. Still others believe it is the ghost of another miner who watched Indians abduct his wife and children. The light, old-timers say, is the miner's lantern and it will appear nightly until he is reunited with his family.

When it first appeared, the ghost light caused such a panic in the nearby village of Hornet that many natives moved away. It was an evil light, the people believed, responsible for a sudden rash of unexplained illnesses and deaths.

The ghost light today is not considered an evil so much as an unexplained phenomenon. Scientists have come to study it, the Army Corps of Engineers, high school and university students, ghost hunters. All are mystified. So, too, are the hundreds of tourists who zero in on Devil's Promenade from all parts of the United States to watch the eerie light careening down the road.

Few have been disappointed because the light appears nightly. Some have chased the Spook Light in their cars only to see it disappear in the distance. Others have fired rifles into it only to see it fragment into a shower of lights. Others have photographed it — successfully, too. But no one, in all the years that the ghost light has been seen, has been able to destroy, identify or explain it.

Fox fire (luminous marsh gas)? Maybe. And yet

winds fail to disperse the ghost light as they do conventional fox fire. The headlights of cars along nearby Route 66 ricocheting off the hills at some freaky angle? Some say so. (And yet *if* so, why was the light seen long before there were automobiles?) Is the light atmospheric electricity? Some abnormal underground charge? Tests have been made. And all have proved negative.

So the Spook Light burns yet along Devil's Promenade — eerie, evanescent and unexplained.

The Phantom Vaquero
of the Texas Plains

No one . . . no animal . . . had been able to overtake them. Not the fastest Indian pony . . . not the fleetest antelope . . . not even the legendary Pacing White Stallion, whirlwind among Texas mustangs.

They were an awesome pair, the great, black, unbroken horse, frothing at the mouth, lathered with sweat, and the rider he bore, a ramrod-straight vaquero — *headless* — in full Mexican regalia: sheepskin chaps worn light-side out, spurs, a brush-and-briar-torn serape, a bullet-riddled, blood-caked buckskin jacket. Swinging from the saddle horn, wearing still its sombrero, was the disembodied head. It was as ghoulish a sight as Southwest Texas had ever seen.

Whenever the horse and rider sensed that they had been spotted, they would thunder off as if possessed, raising clouds of red dust searing across the prickly pear flats, burning up the mesquite grasses, vaulting canyons and arroyos as though each was nothing more than a ditch.

There were legends, of course, about the superhuman rider and satanic horse — Comanche legends, Mexicans legends, cowboy legends. In all, there must have been a dozen different stories to account, in one way or another, for the mysterious pair who during the mid-nineteenth century, shortly after the Mexican War, ranged far and wide over the rock-strewn Texas prairies.

Who *was* the headless horseman? Some said he was the ghostly guard of the lost mine of the deserted Candelaria Mission on the Nueces River. Others believed he was an Indian decoy sent out to frighten cowboys away from the mustang herds, which the Comanche considered their property. Still others insisted the rider was none other than the devil himself.

Each time the pair was sighted, new stories refueled the old, then raced like prairie fire from camp to camp along the Nueces and down across the Mexican border.

There was no special time or place the horse and headless vaquero would appear. They might be seen in the shimmery heat of midday scaling a rough canyon break, or silhouetted against the copper disc of a dying sun, or galloping at dusk across the cactus-lands. They might also be seen in the deep of night, cresting a grassy knoll under a full moon. Always they were the same — the rider so bolt upright in the saddle he might have been spiked to it, the awful head in its battered sombrero dangling from the saddle horn, the untamed horse, wilder than any mustang seen in those parts, bucking, snorting, pawing the air.

Neither horse nor rider seemed to tire. And unlike the mustang herds (always a stallion and his band of mares) that sniffed out a relatively small territory, then confined themselves to it, these two roamed the length of the canyon country, never lingering in one place. They ranged upriver, downriver, crossriver, forever damned to moving on . . . and on . . . and on. Other mustangs shunned them. Whole herds, sometimes, would stampede with tornado fury at sight or scent of them. Men, too, kept their distance.

No one dared move too close, a difficult feat anyhow because of the black mustang's incredible speed and power. Those who ventured within pistol range swore that their bullets passed through the headless figure as easily as through paper, that he remained bolt upright in the saddle, apparently unscathed, unharmed.

Finally, a half-dozen frontiersmen schemed to capture the mustang and headless vaquero, to end forever the mystery. They ambushed the mighty horse at Bull Head, watering on the Nueces, and shot him down. As they closed in, they saw to their horror that the vaquero was indeed headless, a dried-up Mexican cadaver, riddled with bullets, lashed to horse and saddle so tightly that the ropes had to be cut to unfasten it. Tied inside the misshapen sombrero was the head, parched, shrunken, with eyes rotted into the skull.

Half the mystery was solved. But not the corpse's identity. Or the reason for its being lashed to the back of the mustang. Eventually the body was identified as that of a Mexican deserter named Vidal who had fled to Texas with valuable information shortly before the Battle of San Jacinto. After the battle, which settled for a time the war between Texas and Mexico, Vidal remained in Texas, a cattle rustler and horse thief with a price on his head.

Horse thievery in those days was tantamount to murder. Vidal had to be stopped. So the ranchers whose herds Vidal consantly raided banded together, tracked him to his camp, then swooped in at night as he lay sleeping. They shot Vidal, beheaded him and then — perhaps as a warning to other horse thieves — strapped his body to the back of a mighty, unbroken, black stallion, one of the recaptured herd. They then tied Vidal's severed head inside his sombrero and laced it to the saddle horn.

The black mustang, terrified by the scent of fresh blood, reeled across the canyon, pitching, snorting, whinnying, unable to rid himself of his terrible burden. For months . . . years . . . he roamed, bound to — bedeviled by — the dead man on his back.

But at last his life was ended. And with it the mystery of the headless vaquero was laid to rest. Or *was* it?

The canyon country of Southwest Texas is vast, lonesome and eerie, especially at night when coyotes wail and stands of cactus assume the ghostly shapes of men and beasts. The land has changed little since the days of Vidal. Cowboys still ride herd through the canyons and flats, camping at night by chaparral thickets.

And there are those among them who swear that on moonlight nights a black stallion can be seen streaking across the horizon, its rider bolt upright in the saddle . . . its rider headless.

The Galloping Ghost of Laramie

A ghost on an Army post? Fort Laramie, Wyoming, claims one, a lady ghost who gallops a spirited black horse down the old Oregon Trail once every seven years. Who is she? Where did she come from? Here's the story old-timers tell.

A hundred years ago or so, a young West Point graduate, Lieutenant Allison by name, was ordered to Fort Laramie on the prairies of eastern Wyoming. The fort in those days was the most important military outpost on three of the six major wagon trails that crossed Wyoming on their way west: the Oregon, California and Mormon trails. For forty-one years the United States Cavalry rode out of Fort Laramie to assist wagon trains as they lumbered on toward the Great Divide and Rockies, to protect them from outlaws, Indians and untoward acts of nature.

Lieutenant Allison, an Easterner and avid sportsman, had brought with him to Fort Laramie his own hunting dog and his own horse, a prize, high-

stepping thoroughbred. The Wyoming prairies swarmed with game, large and small. Buffalo roamed so close to the fort, it was said, that an officer firing a six-pounder into a herd one day dropped thirty with a single shot. Pheasants, geese, ducks, pronghorn antelope and mule deer were abundant. Beaver, too, in the North Platte and Laramie Rivers. Their skins, a few decades earlier, had lured trappers into the vast prairie grasslands, had necessitated the building of the stockade-cum-trading post that was to become Fort Laramie.

Shortly after arriving at Fort Laramie, Lieutenant Allison joined some of the officers in a hunt in the hills directly southeast of the fort. Wolf was their quarry.

The dogs caught the scent quickly and the chase was on. Lieutenant Allison's mount streaked away from the others, lost them, and the lieutenant found himself alone in strange territory. The Indians of the area, the lieutenant knew, were not hostile. Squaws lazed about Fort Laramie, cooling themselves in the shade of its adobe walls as their children trotted half-naked across the grounds, zinging arrows at blackbirds.

Lieutenant Allison was also aware, however, that bands of Arapaho, Cheyenne and Sioux made frequent forays into the grasslands beyond the fort. They had come originally to trade furs for dry goods, tobacco and whiskey. But today they were less inclined to be amicable, particularly the Sioux, who were making one last valiant effort to withhold their lands from the whites. The years immediately preceding Lieutenant Allison's arrival had been the prairie's bloodiest. Ranchers had been murdered, large herds driven off, wagon trains ravaged. Fort Laramie was constantly "on alert."

The countryside seemed peaceful enough to Lieutenant Allison at the moment — an ocean of grass rippling westward toward a purple wall of mountains. Here and there a sandstone outcropping, sculpted by wind and water. Buzzards arcing high overhead.

Suddenly he saw her, galloping eastward along the Oregon Trail, a striking young woman in a green velvet riding habit and feathered cap. She rode magnificently; still she would be no match for an Indian party on the prowl.

Lieutenant Allison's thoroughbred overtook her easily. But just as he drew alongside, she took a jeweled riding crop to her great black horse and thundered over the brow of a hill. Lieutenant Allison took chase, but when he crested the hill there was no sign of a girl or her horse, merely miles and miles of empty prairie. He dismounted, squatted to examine the trial. There were no hoofprints.

Had he imagined her? Perhaps . . . but wait. His dog had sensed something, too. He was cowering now and whimpering. Lieutenant Allison comforted the dog, then remounted and galloped top speed back to the fort, his dog hard behind.

That night there was a party at Fort Laramie and Lieutenant Allison fully expected to see the "girl in green." Surely she must belong to the fort, be the wife or sweetheart or daughter of someone there. But she was *not* there. Nor was there talk of anyone's being missing as there most certainly would have been had she belonged to the fort and failed to return.

Who was she then? Where did she come from? Did others know her?

He began telling the story of his strange encounter, half expecting to be made fun of. But no jeers or jokes were forthcoming. Only silence.

"Well, Allison," said Fort Laramie's commanding officer after a minute or so. "You have seen the Laramie Ghost."

"Laramie Ghost?" Lieutenant Allison almost laughed. So beautiful a girl a ghost? The horse, too?

The commandant nodded. "She was the daughter of one of the post's first factors," he began. "Thirty-five or forty years ago when it was a fur trading post. Beaver was the thing then . . . made a lot of people rich.

"Anyhow, this post manager brought his daughter with him to Fort Laramie — Fort William, it was then. She was a great beauty, a skilled horsewoman, had a fine black gelding, which she used to race across the prairie.

"One day the factor left on a trip. His last words to his daughter were not to leave the fort unless one of his assistants rode with her. The girl was stubborn. Spoiled, too, you might say. She vowed to ride *when* she wanted . . . *where* she wanted. If it wasn't convenient for one of the post to accompany her, so be it. She would go alone.

"And that's just what happened. She galloped out of the post one afternoon, headed east down the Oregon Trail and was never seen again.

"For weeks the factor searched for his daughter. He must have covered every square inch of ground between here and Torrington. But he never found a trace of the girl or the horse.

"A couple of years later some of the Oglala began to talk about a white woman on a black horse, a spirit-woman who galloped across the prairie at breakneck speed, not regularly, but often enough that she became a sort of legend among them. Several of the soldiers saw her too, or said they did.

"But you're the first to see her in a long time . . . the seven years must be up . . . she rides, you see, only once every seven years now. Just why, no one knows . . ."

Fascinating, this story the commandant told. But was it anything more? Lieutenant Allison believed there must be a logical explanation for "the girl in green." He couldn't, in all seriousness, accept the ghost story. Still, there was the matter of hoofprints — or rather the lack of them, as though that great horse had never touched the ground. And what about the dog? What accounted for his cowering and whimpering? He usually was fearless.

In the days that followed, Lieutenant Allison began making inquiries. He learned that an aging Oglala squaw had seen the girl ride out of Fort Laramie that fateful afternoon. He tracked down the old woman, asked her to describe the girl as she had last seen her.

"Green dress," the woman rasped in a voice so low and husky he could scarcely understand her. "Hat of feathers . . . whip with handle of flashing stones . . . great black horse . . ."

The very girl he had seen . . . *forty years* after her mysterious disappearance.

The girl who is still seen *a hundred and forty years* after her mysterious disappearance, who will next be seen (if she keeps her seven-year schedule) in 1976 . . . on the old Oregon Trail . . . galloping east.

Eerie Iron Horse of the Arizona Desert

Had he *actually* heard it? The *chuff-chuff . . . click-clack . . . chuff-chuff . . . click-clack* of a train? He'd swear to it. Yet, how could that be? Here he was — lost — in the middle of the alkali flats, that vast dead man's land that stretched north from the Dragoon Mountains of southeastern Arizona to the town of Willcox.

There were no trains for miles and miles. Never had been. Just endless, white-hot dust rippling toward a mauve fence of mountains. Nothing lived in this killer land. No, there were no trains here. No reason to be.

He must be crazy with the heat. It was 120° in the shade . . . *Shade!* . . that was a laugh! If only there *was* shade.

How long had he been traveling? Crossing these flats? Was it just yesterday that he'd left Tombstone? Seemed a hundred years ago. Was it only last night the mountain lion had jumped and killed his burro? Or was that last week? Was it an hour ago he'd drained his canteen, then flung it steaming into the sand? Or had that been ten minutes ago?

The heat curdled his brain, scrambled his thoughts, stretched seconds into eternity. He *must* push on . . . *hang* on. If he could only hold out until dark, he could make it. The infernal sun was what drove men mad, burning down, bouncing off the snowy alkali flats as off an ice floe, crazing the earth, crazing men's minds.

He was young, though. And sturdy. And wise to the ways of the desert. Hadn't he been prospecting in these parts for ten years? Hadn't he hit a couple of strikes? Small ones, it was true. Still, he'd felt the weight of gold in his pockets.

Gold was what he was after now. The lucky strike. The big one. The El Dorado. And Doz Cabezas, some fifty miles northeast of Tombstone, was where he hoped to find it.

He'd left Tombstone early of a morning in order to sneak across the Dragoon Mountains by day. This was Apache country. *Cochise* country. The old chief was dead now . . . this was the late 1870s so it must have been five years ago or more that he'd died. Still, there was talk that his spirit hovered about Stronghold Canyon where his hideout had been. And it was a known fact that when the Apache went up into the Dragoons each year to gather *beyotas* (Spanish acorns, which were their favorite food), they left those in Stronghold Canyon unharvested.

They were for the spirit of their great warrior chief.

It wouldn't do to chance meeting any haints. Especially the haint of Cochise. Since it was a whole lot less likely to go a'haunting in broad daylight, he'd left Tombstone about dawn. That way he'd be safely over the mountains by late afternoon, have time for a brief rest before setting out across the flats.

The flats had to be crossed by night. Very few men ever made it by day, as the flats themselves quickly testified: they were littered with skulls and skeletons and the bare bones of wagons incinerated by the midday heat.

He, certainly, had had no intention of being here under the burning sun. But his burro had been killed and that was what had set him behind schedule.

Was the sun lower now? It seemed so. If only he could hold out until dark . . . keep moving . . . slow and easy. Wouldn't do to panic. That was what killed men.

He heard it again. Plain as anything. *Chuff . . . chuff . . . chuff . . . clickety-clack . . . clickety-clack . . . chuff . . . chuff . . . chuff . . .*

It was a train all right. But *where* in tarnation? He squinted across the smoldering sands. They shimmered, danced, then rose up in a mighty blue wave, heaved and broke across the flats.

Whoa there, Johnny, he said to himself. Hold on. He wasn't so far gone he didn't know a mirage when he saw it. And he wasn't about to be fooled as others had been fooled, bumbling blindly toward the giant cool wet lake. No, sir.

There wasn't any water on these flats. It was a trick of the heat that put the lake there. He'd rest easy till the sun set, then be on his way.

What was it he heard now? A clanging? Sounded like a train's bell. There followed a rumbling, then a chugging. Far out on the horizon he saw it, a black speck no bigger than an ant.

Johnny shuddered. The ghost train! That was what he was seeing — the ghost train! He'd heard tell of it around campfires at night. Plenty of folks had seen it on these same flats — settlers, prospectors, rustlers, Mexicans, Apache. And now him. The train just roared up out of nowhere, thundered across the desert lake, then vanished. No one knew why.

Johnny slumped in the sand, eyes mere slits in the glare, watching the black dot hurtle forward across the great blue lake that washed over the flats. It was an old train, from the looks of it. An engine, two bright yellow cars. The stack, squat and fat, coughed up clouds of black smoke and the cow-catcher plowed through the lake like the prow of a riverboat, spreading V-shaped ripples east and west.

On and on the train raced, aiming, it seemed, straight at Johnny. He could see the headlight now — a giant yellow eye burning through the quivery heat. He could see also the engineer, soot blackened, pumping the whistle.

"Whoo-eeeee!" it screeched.

Gotta move, Johnny said to himself. Gotta get outa here before that train mows me down. But he couldn't move. The sun had burned every ounce of energy out of him.

There came a fierce blast of the whistle, a screaming of brakes, a deep, wheezing sigh as the engine came to rest not five feet from where Johnny crouched. Hands reached down, yanked him up and inside a car.

Someone stretched him out in the aisle. He could feel metal, cold under his cheek. He heard voices droning . . . saw faces swim in and out of focus . . .

"Wa-ter," he croaked . . . "please lemme have some water . . ." He wasn't sure he spoke . . . the fires of hell seemed to burn inside his throat.

The engine shuddered, then creaked slowly forward. Seconds later, the train was whizzing again across the desert lake . . . *chuff-chuff* . . . *clack-clack* . . . *chuff-chuff* . . . *clack-clack*. Its rhythm rocketed Johnny into a deep sleep.

A cool trickle of water roused him — someone was wetting his parched lips. Johnny raised up, saw that he was in a large room, saw that the man standing over him wore the silver badge of a sheriff.

"A coupl'a hours more and you'd of been done for," the sheriff said. "Markham here," he jerked his thumb toward another man standing nearby, "found

you on the flats five miles out of Willcox . . . plumb
loco, you was, with the heat . . ."

"The train . . . ?" Johnny squeaked. "The train
. . . ?"

"Train? Ain't no train hereabouts. Ain't none for
miles and miles . . ."

Johnny knew different. He'd heard it, seen it,
owed his life to it.

Old-timers around Tombstone still tell the story of
the ghost train. Many a man, they'll tell you, has
seen it thunder across the alkali flats. Many a man
has heard its low-moaning whistle . . . its *chuff-
chuff* engine . . . its *clickety-clack* wheels . . .

But no one, they add, ever *rode* the ghost train —
no one, that is, except Johnny.

The Mansion of the Dead

In the Santa Clara Valley just south of San Francisco there stands a five-million-dollar mansion, empty, unfurnished and uninhabited — except by spirits of the dead. It is Winchester House, a rambling architectural nightmare built entirely for ghosts, and its bizarre story begins about a hundred years ago in New Haven, Connecticut.

During the latter part of the nineteenth century, the name of Winchester was synonymous with "rifle" and it is with that family that this story deals, specifically with Sarah Winchester, who was married to the son and heir of the "Rifle King." No one knows whether Sarah Winchester was born with "second sight," that is, the ability to communicate with those beyond the grave, or whether she developed that faculty after tragedy struck.

Tragedy did strike Sarah Winchester — a swift, double blow. Within a few short months she lost not only her husband but also her only child. And, it seemed to friends, her sanity as well. Sarah withdrew

behind shuttered windows and doors, growing, as the weeks passed, more and more morbid. When the physicians she consulted were unable to cure or comfort her, she retreated into the spiritual world. She invited mediums into her home, hoping that through seances she could be reunited with her dead husband, William, and with her daughter. Time and again mediums came. And went, without having established contact with William. Sarah then heard about a remarkable medium in Boston named Adam Coons who had had particular success contacting the departed. Sarah went anonymously to Coons, who told her that her husband was standing beside her.

"Tell him that I miss him desperately," she said.

"He wants you to know that he is with you and that he will always be with you," Coons replied. Then he gave Sarah a message from the spirit world that would change her life completely.

"This is a warning," the medium said in a voice that seemed to waft on the air. "You will be haunted forever by the ghosts of those who have been killed by Winchester rifles unless you make amends to them . . ."

She was to sell her New Haven home, move west, and buy there a new home, which her dead husband, William, would point out. She was to rebuild the house, "making room in it for all these spirits." As long as Sarah continued to build, Coons added, she would live — with William nearby.

The seance so moved Sarah that she returned to New Haven at once, sold her property and journeyed cross-country to California. Here she wandered for weeks, searching the towns and countryside, the mountains and valleys, forests and deserts for the house that William wanted. Money was no problem — Sarah had a fortune worth some twenty million dollars and, in addition, an income from the rifle company of about a thousand dollars a day.

Finally, in the peaceful Santa Clara Valley, Sarah found a modest eight-room house on forty-four acres of farmland. "This is it," a disembodied voice said. And she knew that William had spoken.

Sarah bought the farm, then set about her strange task of rebuilding and enlarging, making space for the hundreds of ghosts of those killed by Winchester rifles. She hired eighteen servants and an army of carpenters, plumbers, plasterers, masons, painters and glaziers. For thirty-six years these workmen and artisans followed Sarah Winchester's erratic commands, building up and tearing down, altering and rearranging rooms, wings and ells so that in the end the house sprawled over six acres of ground. Year after year, seven days a week, they toiled. One craftsman spent thirty years building cupolas. Another devoted thirty-three years to laying parquet floors and ripping them up again.

The sound of hammers and saws never ceased as rooms were tacked onto rooms, wings flung out at odd angles, stairways aimed into thin air. There were, finally, two thousand doors (many of which opened onto blank walls), one hundred and sixty rooms, forty-seven fireplaces, forty staircases, dozens of cul-de-sacs, cubbyholes and secret passageways.

As the work progressed, Sarah became obsessed with the number thirteen. She required that each chandelier contain thirteen lights, each ceiling thirteen panels, each room thirteen windows, each stair thirteen steps (there is an exception, however, a stairway which, unaccountably, is divided into seven flights and forty-four steps although it climbs only ten feet from one floor to the next).

During her thirty-six years at Winchester House, Sarah received three famous visitors: President Theodore Roosevelt, who had been a close friend of her husband's; Mary Baker Eddy, the founder of the Christian Science Church; and Harry Houdini, the magician and escape artist. Her most honored guests, however, were the ghosts for whom she was building Winchester House. For them she built a windowless seance room, a small and secret chamber called the Blue Room.

Each midnight, clad in long robes, Sarah retreated to the Blue Room to receive her spiritual companions who were summoned by the tolling of a tower bell. Sarah also gave dinner parties for a dozen carefully chosen phantom guests (always twelve so that with Sarah there were thirteen at table). The menus were lavish, four- and five-course feasts prepared by master chefs whom Sarah had brought over from Paris and Vienna. The banquets continued year after year, attended by guests only Sarah could see.

In September 1922, at the age of eighty-five, Sarah passed into the world of spirits she both loved and feared. She left Winchester House to a niece with strict instructions that her guests of years past continue to be welcome. Later, when the niece sold the house, Sarah's wishes were made a condition of the sale.

Her wishes are honored yet and Winchester House is kept in good repair. By day it is a tourist attraction. Guides tour small groups through a portion of the house, cautioning them "to stay close." Most of the rooms, however, are sealed.

They belong to Sarah and to the night.

The Mystery of Bigfoot

For decades explorers have searched in vain for the Abominable Snowman, that huge, white furry creature that inhabits the Himalayas — or at least the imaginations of the remote mountain people who live there. Now comes a mystery equally baffling, yet much closer to home: Bigfoot.

The thought of such a monster living in twentieth-century America, skulking through the evergreen wilderness of the Pacific Northwest, is difficult to accept. But accept it one must. The beast has been seen, tracked and photographed.

What — who — *is* Bigfoot? A throwback to prehistoric days? A holdout from the Stone Age? Some strange reincarnation? A ghost?

No one can say, any more than he can explain why Bigfoot has chosen to haunt the dense cathedral-quiet forests of Skamania County, Washington, along the banks of the Columbia River.

Nearly everyone around Skamania County believes at least a little bit in Bigfoot. His footprints, they will tell you, measure seventeen inches in length. He covers the ground four feet at a stride. He weighs, very possibly, as much as a quarter of a ton.

Bigfoot is no newcomer. He may be, in fact, centuries old. Long before the memory of white man, Northwest Coast Indian legends told of a towering, hairy giant who lived in nearby forests. Adding luster to these legends were reports, years later, from explorers, trappers and prospectors who had penetrated the Pacific Northwest wilderness. Along the escarpments of the Columbia River, they said, they had seen fresh footprints twice as big as a man's. The first written record of these tracks was entered in a trapper's journal in 1810. As far as is known, the first white man to *see* the beast was a representative of the Hudson's Bay Company. The year was 1864.

It was a Gargantuan creature he saw, well over nine feet tall, all covered with hair. He walked upright like a man, but hunched, with massive hands almost dragging the ground.

Recently, Bigfoot's appearances have been more and more frequent. And he appears to be roaming farther and farther afield from the Columbia River banks. In 1969 alone there were thirty-seven different sightings — from the Cascade Range in Northern California through the Crater Lake country of Oregon to the spruce and fir forests of Washington — a range of some five hundred miles over exceptionally rugged terrain.

Campers in the wilds of Bigfoot Country have reported not only seeing Bigfoot but also of hearing eerie, forbidding sounds in the night: bone-numbing shrieks, long, agonizing wails, muffled sniffling.

But Bigfoot himself remains elusive, slipping in and out of the shadows. And no one knows for sure what he is, who he is, although scientists have scrutinized his footprints and measured them to the nearest micron.

What *is* known is that somewhere out there, deep in the woods, along the river banks, there lives an awesome monster of this world or another, of this life or another.

Ghostly Goddess of the Volcano

His thoughts still with the party he had just left, the young newspaper reporter careened his sports car up Tantalus Mountain road on the Hawaiian island of Oahu. It was two o'clock in the morning and the road, deserted even in midday, snaked mile after mile through a black velvet night, passing neither house nor human being. The headlights danced off the bougainvillea bushes that hedged in the road and off the papaya trees just above them.

It was not a night to believe in ghosts. Or in Hawaii's mischievous dwarfs of the wee hours called Menehunes . . . or in the spectral Night Marchers who were seen sometimes, bathed in a dim unearthly glow, parading on the beach . . . or in . . .

Then he saw her. Far ahead at the bend of the road. A woman in a long, flowing red muumuu, the native dress of the islands. Behind her trotted a little white dog.

The reporter's thoughts raced back to the party, to

a story he had heard about Madame Pele, mysterious goddess of the volcano. What was it someone had said? ". . . she appears just before a volcano erupts . . . she wears a red muumuu . . . there is always a little white dog at her heels . . ."

Could it be? Nonsense. He didn't hold with ghosts or legends or superstitions. The road ahead was empty now. The lady, no doubt, had been an illusion. Probably his headlights striking the scarlet bougainvillea at a freaky angle. Or his eyes playing tricks. It *was* late. The Honolulu party was still very much with him and all of the tales he had heard there.

"My grandfather saw her once, a long time ago," he remembered a doll-like Chinese girl saying. "He was driving his pickup truck and came upon a beautiful woman walking slowly along the side of the road. She was wearing a red muumuu and she had a little white dog.

"My grandfather stopped and offered her a lift. She got in, they drove on for a mile or so, then when my grandfather turned to say something, the woman and the dog were gone. Vanished into thin air. There was no earthly way they could have gotten out of the truck, but they were gone. My grandfather panicked, raced the truck into town, and told the first person he saw on the street what had happened. It was Madame Pele, the man on the street told him. The Goddess of the Volcano. She had come to warn that there would be an eruption . . .

"And do you know that not two days later, there *was* an eruption? Kilauea Crater on the Big Island."

Madame Pele has been appearing and disappearing for centuries, usually on the Big Island of Hawaii, where the volcanic activity is concentrated. Sometimes she is young and beautiful, sometimes old and drawn. Her clothes, however, never change. She always wears a flaming red muumuu. And she is always accompanied by the little white dog.

Madame Pele comes of a distinguished family of Hawaiian gods, and her home originally was the lush green island of Kauai, northernmost of the five major Hawaiian Islands. She moved from that island — no one knows quite why — across Oahu where Honolulu is located, across the island of Molokai with its precipitous cliffs, across the sugarcane fields of Maui, across the pineapple plantations of Lanai until she came, at last, to the Big Island of Hawaii where the peaks of Mauna Loa and Mauna Kea climb so high that their volcanic craters are frosted with snow.

It's said that when Madame Pele reached the slopes of Mauna Loa, she began to dig, day and night, until she had found the molten heart of the mountain. Warmth is what she had been seeking, and once she had found it she made Kilauea Crater on the eastern flank of Mauna Loa her home. As long as the volcano was quiescent, Madame Pele lived there happily. But whenever the cauldrons deep within began to simmer, Madame Pele came down from the mountain to roam, to warn, islanders believe, of impending disaster.

These were the thoughts that spun through the reporter's head as he nosed his little car into a hairpin curve. Around the bend he saw again the lady in red with the little white dog. His eyes weren't playing tricks. He slowed to get a closer look, and as the lights of his car swept over the lady she turned and seemed ever so slightly to smile. She was young and very beautiful.

Should he offer her a ride? He remembered with a shudder the stories he'd heard of the punishment Madame Pele inflicted upon those who ignored her or were rude or insensitive. Death was in her power, utter destruction, because she could direct the flow of lava.

The reporter hit the brake, leaned over to open the door, but when he looked up to admit the woman, she had vanished. He got out of the car, searched the road, peered deep into the bougainvillea. There was no sign of her or of the dog.

Three days later, Kilauea erupted.

This time it did not confine itself to the firepit. Angry cauldrons bubbled up in a sugar field on the side of Mauna Loa not far from the village of Kapoho. It was a massive eruption. Soon a new crater had formed and Madame Pele's molten fingers rolled forward across green land. They incinerated orchards and cane fields and vaporized a deep, orchid-fringed pool into a terrifying steam cloud.

One by one, as the lava touched them, trees turned into torches and Kapoho's frame houses exploded like matchboxes. One small building was scooped up by the flow and carried, burning, atop the molten mass until it disintegrated into ash.

For days, weeks, the pyrotechnics continued. At night flames leapt 1500 feet into the sky, and lava collided with the surf, raising giant geysers of steam. Some said Pele's silhouette could be seen in the steam clouds sent skyward each time a river of lava reached the sea.

Madame Pele was not altogether merciless during this eruption. She spared, for example, a lighthouse that had stood in the path of the oncoming lava because fishermen, who looked to the lighthouse as their beacon, had knelt in reverence to Pele. She also spared, as she had done during the past, Volcano House that perches directly above Mauna Loa's fire-pit because the inn's owner regularly, and with great ceremony, emptied bottles of gin into the crater to keep Pele happy. Others, seeking Madame Pele's favors, had laid chickens to roast on the rim of the volcano.

Absurd demonstrations by the superstitious? Perhaps. And yet it is not merely the superstitious who have encountered Madame Pele. The young newspaper reporter, certainly, must be counted a skeptic. So, too, must the volcanologists who have come to Hawaii to study eruptions.

Several of these scientists admit to having seen Madame Pele, or at least to having seen, shortly before an eruption, a woman in a flaming red muumuu with a little white dog. They also admit that they have no explanation for her sudden appearances and disappearances. Or for the volcanic upheaval that follows each of her visitations. And, although doing so is utterly unscientific, they are inclined to agree with the natives that if ever a lady in red does appear, trailed by a little white dog, it is best to pay attention. And to show respect.